Ethics without Ontology

ETHICS

without

ONTOLOGY

Hilary Putnam

Harvard University Press
Cambridge, Massachusetts
London, England   2004

Library of Congress Cataloging-in-Publication Data
Putnam, Hilary.
  Ethics without ontology / Hilary Putnam.
    p. cm.
  Includes bibliographical references and index.
  ISBN 0-674-01310-7 (alk. paper)
  1. Ethics.   2. Ontology.   I. Title.
  B945.P873E84 2004
  191–dc22   2003057117

To the memory of my mother,
Riva Putnam

Acknowledgments

Part I of this book was presented as a series of four Hermes lectures (of the same title: "Ethics without Ontology") at the University of Perugia, in October 2001. The idea of my giving them was first raised in May 2000 by Giancarlo Marchetti, Antonio Pieretti, and Carlo Vinti. I once again thank them warmly, not only for the opportunity to lecture on my current interests, but also for introducing me to "the green heart of Italy," the beautiful province of Umbria, and for the wonderful hospitality that every member of the Department of Philosophy showed me. I also want to thank Gemma Corradi-Fiumara for chairing one of my lectures, and for companionship (including the intellectual stimulation I found in reading her fascinating philosophical and psychoanalytic study *The Mind's Affective Life*); I am grateful as well to the student who did so much to make our trip run smoothly and pleasantly, Marco Bastianelli, to whom Ruth Anna and I wish a successful career in philosophy.

In the spring of that same year (2001), I was Baruch de Spinoza Visiting Professor in the Department of Philosophy at the University of Amsterdam, and my Spinoza Lectures, "Enlightenment and Pragmatism," form Part II of this book. My predecessor in the Spinoza Chair, my good friend Seyla Benhabib, wrote in the preface to her Spinoza Lectures, "It was a special honor for me, a Sephardic Jew, as Spinoza was, to hold these lectures under the auspices of a Spinoza chair in his name." I am an Ashkenazi Jew, not a Sephardic one, but I understand very well what she meant. Although my lectures are not about Spinoza, their central question—what enlightenment means—is one that was close to Spinoza's heart. Moreover, during the three months I spent in Amsterdam, I was welcomed to the Sabbath worship services at the "Portuguese-Israelite" synagogue in Amsterdam—ironically, the synagogue from which Spinoza was expelled! (an action the present-day members, needless to say, very much regret)—and I shall always remember and be grateful for the warm fellowship of the congregation, and the deep spirituality of the previously unfamiliar Sephardic ritual in the beautiful space of one of the oldest and largest of the surviving synagogues of Europe. It is strange to think that Spinoza and I have been members of the same *minyan!*

Equally, I shall always remember and be grateful for the warm fellowship of the members of the Philosophy Department of the University of Amsterdam. Not only their company and their hospitality, but their interest in and critical responses to my work were invaluable. I will not list all of them by name, for I felt a real collegiality with all the members of the Department (including the Chairman, Frans Jacobs, and the two wonderful secretaries, Ria Beentjes and Willy van Wier), but I want to thank in particular Hent de Vries, whom I saw just about every day we were both in town, and whose intellectual and personal friendship meant a great deal. I also want to mention two philosophers who are not members of the Amsterdam department, Paula Marati and Herman Philipse, whose companionship and conversation were also a great pleasure.

Finally, I want once again to thank my wife, Ruth Anna Putnam, who more than anyone else brought me to an appreciation of American pragmatism in general, and of the significance of John Dewey's contribution to philosophy in particular.

Contents

Ethics without Ontology

Introduction

It may seem strange that a book with the title *Ethics without Ontology* deals as much or more with issues in the philosophy of logic and the philosophy of mathematics as it does with ethics, but this is no accident. For I believe that the unfortunate division of contemporary philosophy into separate "fields" (ethics, epistemology, philosophy of mind, philosophy of science, philosophy of language, philosophy of logic, philosophy of mathematics, and still others) often conceals the way in which the very same arguments and issues arise in field after field. For example, arguments for "antirealism" in ethics are virtually identical with arguments for antirealism in the philosophy of mathematics; yet philosophers who resist those arguments in the latter case often capitulate to them in the former. We can only regain the integrated vision which philosophy has always aspired to if at least some of the time we allow ourselves to ignore the idea that a philosophical position or argument must deal with one and only one of these specific "fields."

The invitation to give the Hermes Lectures at the University of Perugia (Part I of the present volume) provided me with an opportunity to formulate and present in public something I realized I had long wanted to say, namely that the renewed (and continuing) respectability of Ontology (the capital letter here is intentional!) following the publication of W. V. Quine's "On What There Is" at the midpoint of the last century has had disastrous consequences for just about every part of analytic philosophy. In various essays, in the course of my own half-century's activity as a philosopher, I have touched on related themes, of course. For example, I have claimed that ethics and mathematics can and do possess objectivity without being about sublime or intangible objects, such as "Platonic forms" or "abstract entities," and that the idea that "exist" has a unique and determinate meaning, one cast in stone, so to speak, is mistaken. And ethics, I have argued, following the lead of the classic American pragmatists, must not be identified with one single human concern or with one single set of concepts. But I have never before attempted to show the interrelatedness of this whole group of issues, and that is what I tried to do in this set of lectures.

In doing so, I was subject to the constraint that the lectures were for a large general audience, but I welcomed that constraint because the issues are simply too important to be discussed only in front of specialists. The first lecture, in particular, tries to explain in a non-technical way what I mean by "ontology" and what I mean by "ethics" in the present context. The next two lectures of Part I are more technical, but even here I have tried to explain those technical notions I absolutely had to introduce in as non-technical a way as possible. Lecture 2, on conceptual relativity, explains what I mean by saying that "exist" is a concept that can be and is continually being extended in various ways (consistently with the core examples of its use), and goes on to argue that asking "do numbers really exist?" is asking a question to which Ontologists have not succeeded in giving a sense. (Just saying, "By exist I mean *exist*," and stamping your foot, doesn't do it.) The final lecture of Part I brings together the remarks on ethics in the first lecture and the criticism of the whole idea of Ontology in the second and third, and concludes by pronouncing an obituary on Ontology.

Given both the time constraint of four lectures and the nature of the audience, it would have been neither possible nor appropriate to go into greater detail either on my reasons for rejecting the widespread belief that ethical judgments lack objectivity, or on the philosophy of logic and mathematics. The former are set out in *The Collapse of the Fact/Value Dichotomy* (Harvard University Press, 2002), while some of my publications on the latter are indicated in the notes to the second and third lectures in Part I of the present volume. If there is a common element in my treatment of these two topics, it lies, I think, in this: I see the attempt to provide an Ontological explanation of the objectivity of mathematics as, in effect, an attempt to provide *reasons which are not part of mathematics for the truth of mathematical statements* and the attempt to provide an Ontological explanation of the objectivity of ethics as a similar attempt to provide *reasons which are not part of ethics for the truth of ethical statements*; and I see both attempts as deeply misguided. Seeing that and how they are misguided is an absolute prerequisite to recovering our common sense in these areas. That is what I hope to persuade the reader of in the present volume.

In Part I, John Dewey figures as just one member of my list of "heroes," and I praise him there especially for emphasizing that the function of ethics is not, in the first instance, to arrive at "universal principles." The primary aim of the ethicist, in Dewey's view and in the view I defend, should not be to produce a "system," but to contribute to the solution of practical problems—as, indeed, Aristotle already knew. Although we can often be *guided* by universal principles (at least they are typically stated as if they were universal and exceptionless) in the solution of practical problems, few real problems can be solved by treating them as mere instances of a universal generalization, and few practical problems are such that when we *have* resolved them—and Dewey held that the solution to a problem is always provisional and fallible—we are rarely able to express what we learned in the course of our encounter with a "problematic situation" in the form of a universal generalization that can be unproblematically applied to other situations. Even Kant, who is often considered to be *the* great representative of the sort of ethical theory that seeks to lay down universal moral rules, was well aware that what he called "the moral law" cannot be applied to concrete situations without the aid of what he himself calls "mother wit," and that "mother wit" or "good judgment" is not something that can be reduced to an algorithm.[1]

Dewey is included in my list of "heroes" in Part I for two reasons: (1) to indicate how, in my conception, ethics rests not on a single interest or aim, but on a variety of different interests (I can imagine Dewey saying that, in one way or another, it ultimately rests on *every* human interest), and (2) to illustrate the way in which ethics is (in a term I borrow from Wittgenstein)[2] a "motley." It was not necessary to go into more detail than this about Dewey's thought, or, for that matter, about the thought of any of my "heroes," in Part I because the purpose of the Hermes Lectures was to criticize certain fallacious conceptions—conceptions linking ontology, metaphysics, and the theory of truth—that, in my view, have had deleterious effects on our thinking as much in philosophy of logic and philosophy of mathematics as in ethics. When I decided to publish these lectures in the present volume, however, it seemed advisable to add to them, as Part II, "Enlightenment and Pragmatism," the Spinoza Lectures I delivered under that title in Amsterdam in the spring of 2001, which give a picture, albeit a brief one, of my "positive" ethical thinking, and which, moreover, set the problems of ethics in a historical context which not only leads up to but very much includes our present-day situation.

I describe that context with the aid of the idea that there was not just one single "enlightenment," the Enlightenment with a capital "E" that we associate with the seventeenth and eighteenth centuries, but *three* enlightenments, the third of which—which has not yet come fully to fruition—I associate with the name of John Dewey. (The first enlightenment I describe is associated with Plato and Socrates.)

"Enlightenments," in my sense, are simultaneously revolutions in our epistemological thinking and in our ethical thinking. It is uncontroversial—or as uncontroversial as any saying can be in this area—that we ought to use intelligence in trying to resolve ethical and political problems. But it is characteristic of the thinkers who begin an enlightenment that they tell us that we have never, in fact, understood that truism properly; that we do not, in fact, know what it is to apply intelligence to an ethical or political problem. Enlightenment thinkers, in rethinking what it is to use intelligence in dealing with ethical and political problems, typically propose revisions, "reforms," in the ways we deal with many of those problems. In the first of the two lectures that make up Part II (the second is devoted to rebutting contemporary skepticism about the very notion of "enlightenment"), I describe how this was the case with the Platonic enlightenment and in the Enlightenment with a capital "E," and, in more detail, how it is the case with the proposed Deweyan enlightenment.

Although Dewey agrees with the seventeenth- and eighteenth-century Enlightenment thinkers that just governments must have the consent of those governed, he differs with some of the most famous Enlightenment thinkers—in particular with Rousseau and Kant—in utterly rejecting the idea that we should think of society as based upon a "social contract." What is even more striking is that a substantial amount of Dewey's writing (for example, *The Quest for Certainty*) is devoted to unmasking empiricism. What I mean by "unmasking empiricism" is showing how both empiricism and its favorite moral theory, Utilitarianism, while paying lip service to fallibilism, are actually dogmatic. In Dewey's view, classical empiricism and rationalism are, in a way, mirror images of each other; rationalists claimed that they could determine *a priori* some of the most fundamental natural laws (the laws of geometry and mechanics), while empiricists claimed to determine once and for all the form that the *data* for *any* scientific theory must have. (They believed they could do this by means of empiricism's sensationalistic epistemology—an epistemology that was, in fact, alive and well in philosophy of science throughout the first half of the twentieth century, and served to corrupt much of the philosophy of physics that was produced by the Logical Positivists.)[3] In fact, empiricism was not only dogmatic without admitting that it was, but—and this quite consciously—it was reductionistic as well. Indeed, Reductionism was one of the central dogmas of empiricism, as Quine noted (if only in a limited way) in his famous mid-century critical essay, "Two Dogmas of Empiricism."

The great empiricist philosopher in the nineteenth century who most shared Dewey's passion for social reform and Dewey's concern with applying scientifically disciplined intelligence to the problems of social reform was John Stuart Mill. (In many ways, Dewey's *Logic* was a reply to Mill's *A System of Logic*,[4] and in particular to the vision of social inquiry in that work.)[5] What Mill's traditional empiricist beliefs—in particular, Mill's reductionism—led him to, in Dewey's view, was not a workable program for social inquiry. Rather, Mill fabulated a form of social science that does not exist and is not likely to exist in the foreseeable future, if ever: an imaginary social science in which "laws of society" are deduced from a perfected individual psychology.

The fact that Dewey was concerned with epistemology as well as with social reform, and with the interrelationship of the two, has led to significant misunderstandings of his philosophy. Dewey was not simply a social activist[6] calling for democratic reforms and for research—fallibilistic, non-reductionist research—into the causes of social problems and into the ways in which reform was most likely to be successful in resolving them, although he was certainly *at least* that. Like Kant, Dewey was a great aesthetician as well as a great moral philosopher and a great epistemologist,[7] and—as is the case with Kant—it is impossible to understand Dewey's thought properly without understanding the profound links that Dewey saw between these three subjects. These links were not the subject of the lectures in Part II, but I can, perhaps, give some idea of their nature by saying that what is common to Dewey's aesthetic writing and to Dewey's ethical writing, just as it is common to Kant's aesthetic writing and Kant's moral writing, is a complex vision of human nature. (That vision is most fully set out in Dewey's *Human Nature and Conduct*, although its main features are already apparent in the 1908 edition of the *Ethics*.)[8] Here I have space to mention only one aspect: Dewey's account of moral motivation.

In Part II, I point out that, unlike Kant, Dewey entirely rejects the idea that there is a separate and unique moral motivation. (In the Kantian inflection of that idea, the moral motivation is a complicated one: the desire to fully manifest the fact that I am a rational being with free will by freely giving myself a law, one which, according to Kant, is the only possible moral law that every free and rational being can give itself simply *out of the desire to give itself a law that every free and rational being can give itself*.)[9] But Dewey also rejects the Benthamite idea that there is a single natural impulse, the impulse of Sympathy, which, when combined with reflection and impartiality, can give rise to all of ethics. Thus, in the 1908 *Ethics* we find Dewey writing:

What is required is a blending, a fusing of the sympathetic tendencies with all the other impulses and habitual traits of the self. When interest in power is permeated with an affectionate impulse, it is protected from being a tendency to dominate and tyrannize; it becomes an interest in effectiveness of regard for common ends. When an interest in artistic or scientific objects is similarly fused, it loses the indifferent and coldly impersonal character which marks the specialist as such, and becomes an interest in the adequate aesthetic and intellectual development of the conditions of a common life. Sympathy does not merely associate one of these tendencies with another; still less does it make one a means to the other's ends. It so intimately permeates them as to transform both into a new and moral interest.[10]

And he concludes the section by telling us that what is needed is "sympathy transformed into a habitual standpoint which satisfies the demand for a standpoint which will render the person interested in foresight of all obscure consequences" (as opposed to the untransformed natural instinct of sympathy to which Bentham appealed).[11]

What Dewey found objectionable in the Kantian account is not only the transcendental metaphysics of Freedom that Kant presupposes, but the dualism of acting on my "pure reason" as a free being and acting on "inclination" (the second representing merely our animal nature and the former our immortal soul) that runs through that metaphysics, at least in the *Critique of Practical Reason*.[12] Thus Dewey writes,

It is impossible to draw any fixed line between the content of the moral good and of natural satisfaction. The end, the right and only right end, of man, lies in the fullest and freest realization of powers in their appropriate objects. The good consists of friendship, family and political relations, economic utilization of mechanical resources, science, art, in all their complex and variegated forms and elements. There is no separate and rival moral good; no separate empty and rival "good will."[13]

Yet Kant's Categorical Imperative in its more familiar form (act only on such maxims as you would be willing to universalize) is not by any means useless, in Dewey's view. As he writes,

> As a method (though not of course the only one) of realizing the full meaning of a proposed course of action, nothing could be better than asking ourselves how we should like to be committed forever to its principle: how we should like to have others committed to it, and to treat us according to it? . . . In short, by generalizing a purpose, we make its general character evident.
>
> But this method does not proceed (as Kant would have it) from a mere consideration of the moral law apart from a concrete end, but from an end insofar as it persistently approves itself to reflection after an adequate survey of it in all its bearings.[14]

I believe that Dewey's perceptive and realistic refusal to reduce ethics to a single biological trait (such as sympathy) or to any single concern or to any one rule or system of rules, coupled, as it was, with his insistence that nonetheless intelligence—*situated* intelligence—is both possible and necessary in the resolution of political and ethical problems, makes him particularly relevant to our time. However, I find that when I talk about Dewey, either in public lectures or in classes, the question that constantly comes up is whether Dewey is not "too optimistic." But this charge entirely misses the nature of Deweyan optimism. As Dewey himself explained it:

> The good can never be demonstrated to the senses, nor be proved by calculations of personal profit. It involves a radical venture of the will in the interest of what is unseen and prudentially incalculable. But such optimism of will, such determination of the man that, so far as his choice is concerned, only the good shall be recognized as real, is very different from a sentimental refusal to look at the realities of the situation just as they are. In fact a certain intellectual pessimism, in the sense of a steadfast willingness to uncover sore points, to acknowledge and search for abuses, to note how presumed good often serves as a cloak for actual bad, is a necessary part of the moral optimism which actively devotes itself to making the right prevail. Any other view reduces the aspiration and hope, which are the essence of moral courage, to a cheerful animal buoyancy; and, in its failure to see the evil done to others in its thoughtless pursuit of what it calls good, is next door to brutality, to a brutality bathed in the atmosphere of sentimentality and flourishing the catchwords of idealism.[15]

Dewey was not someone with a blind faith in progress; he was, rather, a *strategic optimist;*[16] and strategic optimism is something we badly need at the present time.

Still, I was aware, when I wrote the lectures in Part II, that speaking of "enlightenment" today is like waving a red flag at a bull, or at a number of different bulls, and for that reason, in the final lecture (of both Part II and this volume) I review and reply to prominent critics of the very idea of enlightenment, both in the camp of continental philosophy and in the camp of analytic philosophy.

PART I

Ethics without Ontology

Ethics without Metaphysics

About forty years ago my famous colleague Willard van Orman Quine, who, alas, passed away in December 2000, heard a talk at Harvard by a famous philosopher (whom I shall not name). Quine was asked afterwards what he thought of the talk, and in his beautifully civilized way he said very gently, "He paints with a broad brush." Then he paused, and less kindly added, "and he thinks with one too!"

In this opening lecture, I too shall be "painting with a broad brush," trying to explain in a very general way what it is that I shall be trying to cover in these four lectures. In subsequent lectures, however, I will use a finer brush.

What Do I Mean by "Ontology"?

The title of this set of lectures (Part I) is "Ethics without Ontology." I know that in Europe (at least in some countries) the word "ontology" is more apt to be associated with Heidegger's "fundamental ontology" than with the traditional inquiry that goes back to Aristotle's *Metaphysics*, or with the particular inflection that contemporary analytic philosophy has given to the notion of ontology since the publication of Quine's famous paper "On What There Is" in 1948. Since, like Heidegger, I am critical of the ontological tradition (although not exactly for his reasons: Heidegger never deigned to learn much about analytic philosophy)—critical, that is, of what Heidegger scorned as "onto-theology"—and, like Heidegger again, I think that philosophy needs to take the ways of thinking that are indispensable in everyday life much more seriously than the onto-theological tradition has been willing to do, it might seem that I must in some way be in Heidegger's camp, or perhaps be approaching some of Heidegger's conclusions from a Wittgensteinian direction. But that isn't what I wish to do in these lectures.

Heidegger was not the only major philosopher in the twentieth century to value the *Lebenswelt*, the "life-world," and to condemn the tendency of metaphysicians (including some metaphysicians who call themselves "analytic philosophers") to take it less than seriously. Wittgenstein did so as well, as did the American pragmatists, especially John Dewey. Like Dewey's, my own philosophy is strongly falli-bilistic,[1] but like Wittgenstein, and unlike the pragmatists, I think that one of the most difficult things to do in philosophy is to find a way to uphold the truth in fallibilism without giving up the game to skepticism. In particular, I join the pragmatists in utterly rejecting the idea that there is a set of substantive necessary truths that it is the task of philosophy to discover, but I no longer think (as I once did) that it makes sense to affirm, as Quine does, that everything we presently believe can be revised.[2]

All this is a long-winded way of saying that I shall not be using the word "ontology" in Heidegger's sense. Ontology, in the other sense, the more traditional one, is part of metaphysics (at times, for some philosophers, it seems to be virtually the whole of metaphysics), and it is often described as "the science of Being." The most famous philosophers who pursued ontology in this traditional sense might be called "inflationary" ontologists. In ancient philosophy, the most famous example of an inflationary ontologist is the Plato who gave us the Theory of Forms, at least as that theory has been traditionally interpreted.[3] That interpretation has in turn given rise to the term "Platonism" as the name for a particular kind of inflationary ontological view. As this example illustrates, the inflationary ontologist claims to tell us of the existence of things unknown to ordinary sense perception and to common sense, indeed things that are invisible (somewhat as modern physics informs us of the existence of invisible things, except that the invisible things that the classical ontologist tells us about, for example "Platonic Forms," are quite unknown to modern physical science). Moreover, these invisible things which the inflationary ontologist claims to have discovered are supposed to be supremely important. For Plato, in this reading of him, the existence of the Forms, and particularly the Form of the Good, explains the existence of ethical value and obligation. The Theory of Forms purports to tell us what the Good Life really is and what Justice really is (and often much else besides).

Inflationary metaphysics, of course, continues right up to the present period. At the beginning of the twentieth century, for example, G. E. Moore's celebrated *Principia Ethica* announced that what ethical judgments are really about is a single, supersensible quality he called *good*. (Moore called it a "non-natural" quality.) Not only is *good* supposed to be invisible to the senses and undetectable by the natural sciences, it is also "simple," according to Moore's theory—that is, not analyzable in terms of other properties or qualities. In this respect, it was supposed to be like the color yellow, although (as Moore pointed out) yellow is a natural (in fact a sensible) quality, whereas the allegedly unitary and simple quality of *good* is not. And for Moore, just as for the Platonist (although Moore's ethical theory was quite different from any Platonic one), it is by a special intuition of the supersensible object (in Moore's theory, an intuition of which states of affairs possess the greatest amount of *good*) that we determine the correct ethical judgments.

Before I go any farther, let me make a remark by way of orientation. What is wrong with "Platonic" metaphysics, or with G. E. Moore's inflationary metaphysics, by my lights, *isn't* the idea that there are some persons, traits of character, activities, situations, etc., that can correctly be described as "good." And anyone who has read Plato's *Republic* or Moore's *Principia Ethica* knows that there are moments of great and valuable insight into *which* activities, persons, and traits of character are good in those works. I don't for one moment mean to suggest that one cannot learn an enormous amount from the writings of even the most inflationary metaphysicians. But when one thinks that one has explained *why* some persons, traits of character, activities, and states of affairs are good by postulating something "non-natural," something mysterious and sublime standing invisibly behind the goodness of the persons, actions, situations, etc., in question, one thereby commits oneself to a form of *monism* in the sense that one reduces (or imagines one has reduced) all ethical phenomena, all ethical problems, all ethical questions, indeed all value problems, to just *one* issue, the presence or absence of this single super-thing *Good*.

Not surprisingly, ethicists, starting with Aristotle, responded by pointing out that there are *many* questions concerning ethics, not only questions about good but questions about virtue, which cannot be usefully answered by talking about "the Form of the Good,"[4] and, as eighteenth- and nineteenth-century ethicists were to add, questions about duty, questions about obligation, and so on; and the assumption that all the *many* sorts of questions that there are in Ethics can be reduced to one single question is quite unjustified. The idea with which a particular inflationary metaphysician is enchanted may throw real light on some questions, but all the questions outside the circle of light are typically plunged into darkness.

Of course, inflationary metaphysicians do not restrict themselves to ethics; we also have metaphysical explanations of the nature of mathematics, metaphysical explanations of the whole course of history (Hegel), and of much else besides.

Besides inflationary metaphysics, I want now to mention two other, deflationary rather than inflationary, ways of ontologizing that are found in the history of philosophy. I shall call them *reductionism* and *eliminationism*. The reductionist ontologist, as the name suggests, says that "A is nothing but B," or that so-and-sos are nothing but such-and-suches—for example, "goodness is nothing but pleasure" or "properties are nothing but names"; or, coming to more recent versions: "ethical utterances are nothing but expressions of feeling," "physical objects are nothing but logical constructions out of sensations." *Nominalism,* one famous kind of deflationary ontology, was traditionally the denial of the existence of such things as *properties.* Very often it took the reductionist form just described, as in "properties (or 'universals,' as they were called) are nothing but names that we apply to a number of different things." But nominalism may take a different form. Another sort of nominalist may say, "I don't claim that properties *are* general names; I claim that *there aren't* any such things as properties or universals; there are only particular things, including particular names or particular sensations or particular images in the mind." This sort of nominalist is an eliminationist—an eliminationist with respect to properties. Similarly, someone who says the following is an eliminationist—an eliminationist with respect to *good:* "I don't say that good is pleasure, or even long-run pleasure, or the greatest pleasure of the greatest number over the longest time; there *isn't such a thing.* Whenever we call anything good we *make the mistake* of supposing that there is such a property at all."[5] Likewise, someone who says "There aren't any such things as numbers or sets or functions or other 'mathematical entities,' mathematics is a kind of *make-believe*" is an eliminationist—an eliminationist with respect to mathematical objects.[6] In short, the eliminationist, like the reductionist, says that there are *nothing but* so-and-sos, where the so-and-sos are a very small part of what we normally purport to talk about—that is why I refer to both reductionism and eliminationism as *deflationary* ontological strategies—but unlike the reductionist he does not say that this is so because the things we purport to talk about (properties as opposed to names, in the case of the traditional metaphysical debate about "universals"; value, duty, obligation, virtue, etc., in the ethical case; numbers and functions and sets in the mathematical case) are *really* so-and-sos, or that talk about the things we purport to talk about is somehow "reducible" to talk of so-and-sos (to talk of names, or sense data, or pleasure, or elementary particles, for example); he says that our ordinary talk is cognitively just as mistaken as talk of alchemy, or phlogiston, or witches. The reductionist's aim is to show us what we are "really" saying (and that what we are really saying is compatible with his minimalist ontology); the eliminationist's aim is to show us that we are talking about mythical entities. But both are deflationists. Perhaps the two most famous deflationary ontologists in the history of philosophy were Democritus, on the one hand (*There is nothing but atoms and the void*), and Berkeley on the other (*There is nothing but spirits and their ideas,* i.e., minds and their sensations)—and they spawned both reductionist and eliminationist versions of, respectively, materialism and idealism. When in the last of these four lectures I present an obituary on the project of Ontology, it will be an obituary on all of these versions, the deflationary as well as the inflationary.

In place of Ontology (note the capital "O"), I shall be defending what one might call *pragmatic pluralism,* the recognition that it is no accident that in everyday language we employ many different kinds of discourses, discourses subject to different standards and possessing different sorts of applications, with different logical and grammatical fea-

tures—different "language games" in Wittgenstein's sense—
no accident because it is an illusion that there could be just
one sort of language game which could be sufficient for the
description of all of reality!

My pragmatic pluralism may, perhaps, make it clear why I
reject eliminationism in both its materialist, or Demo-
critean, form and its idealist, or Berkleyan, form; but why
will I be rejecting inflationary (for example, "Platonic")
metaphysics? My answer is that I hold, with the pragmatists
and again with Wittgenstein, that pragmatic pluralism does
not require us to find mysterious and supersensible objects
behind our language games; the truth can be told in language games that we actually play when language is working,
and the inflations that philosophers have added to those language games are examples, as Wittgenstein said—using a
rather pragmatist turn of phrase—of "the engine idling."[7]
But since my purpose in this opening lecture is only to indicate how I am using the term "ontology," I will stop here for
the moment.

How I Understand "Ethics"

I am not going to understand "ethics" as the name of a system of principles—although principles (for example, the
Golden Rule, or its sophisticated successor, the Categorical
Imperative) are certainly a part of ethics—but rather as a
system of interrelated concerns, concerns which I see as mutually supporting but also in partial tension. When I use it
without "shudder quotes," I shall not give the word "ethics"
such a wide sense as to say, with "sociobiologists," for example, that "ethics" is present in all human cultures because in

all cultures there are individuals who are prepared to sacrifice for the survival of the community. The human capacity for loyalty to something larger than the individual, something at least as large as the community, is indeed a *presupposition* of ethics, as I shall be using the term, but the exercise of that capacity is compatible, for example, with an "ethics" (note the shudder quotes!) that sees (*not* concern for the welfare of others but) courage and "manly prowess" as the chief virtues. The glorification of warfare and *machismo* may, indeed, be older in the history of human cultures than the emphasis on alleviating suffering regardless of the class or gender of the sufferer, but it is this latter outlook, which has deep roots in the great religious traditions of the world—not in only the religious traditions of the West, but in Islam, Confucianism, Hinduism, and Buddhism as well—to which I shall refer by the name "ethics." In fact, what I call "ethics" is precisely the morality that Nietzsche deplored, and regarded as a weakness or even a sickness (which is not to accuse Nietzsche of thinking that an ethics of machismo and physical courage would today be anything but a ridiculous throwback).

While there are an indefinitely large number of concerns that have come to be associated with ethics in this sense—the ethics of compassion, especially since the rise of modern democracy—I can perhaps best indicate at least some of the central concerns, perhaps the most central, by mentioning the names of three philosophers, though in reverse historical order: Levinas, Kant, and Aristotle. I mention Levinas first because my title, "Ethics without Ontology," could well have been the title of one of Levinas's works. The theme at the center of Levinas's philosophy is, indeed, that all attempts to reduce ethics to a theory of being, or to base ethics upon a theory of being, upon ontology, *either* in the traditional sense or in the Heideggerian sense, are disastrous failures.[8] For Levinas, the irreducible foundation of ethics is *my* immediate recognition, when confronted with a suffering fellow human being, that *I* have an obligation to do something. To be sure, as Levinas is well aware, none of us can help all of the other suffering human beings, and the obligation to help a particular human being may be overridden by the obligation to help what he calls "the third." But not to feel the obligation to help the sufferer at all, not to recognize that if I can, I *must* help, or to feel that obligation only when the suffering person I am confronted with is *nice,* or *sympathetic,* or *someone I can identify with,* is not to be ethical at all, no matter how many principles one may be guided by or willing to give one's life for.[9]

I mentioned Kant. To be sure, my attack on inflationary ontology can be seen as being in a Kantian spirit, for Kant was, of the great modern philosophers, the first to renounce the traditional metaphysical project of describing the world as it is "in itself," that is to say, precisely the project of ancient, as well as contemporary, ontology. But Kant we might describe as being an inflationary ontologist *contre lui,* for, although he renounces the traditional project of ontology, he does so on the basis of a theory of the powers of the mind— a theory which is supposedly *prior* to metaphysics, but which (as Hegel already saw) is riddled with metaphysics through and through. All of Kant's fundamental psychological distinctions—for example, his sharp separation (at least in the first and second *Critique*) of Reason and Inclination, and his belief that someone guided by Inclination is simply subject to deterministic forces, while someone guided by Reason will *ipso facto* want to live by rules which any "rational" person could legislate for him- or herself—are, indeed, perfect examples of what I have been calling "inflationary ontology." However, this is not the side of Kant I want to praise. It is rather the Categorical Imperative (not, indeed, as a practical guide—as a guide it scarcely goes beyond the Golden Rule—but as a powerful statement of the idea that ethics is *universal,* that, insofar as ethics is concerned with the alleviation of suffering, it is concerned with the alleviation of *everyone's* suffering, or if it is concerned with positive well-being, it is concerned with *everybody's* positive well-being) that I think is Kant's great achievement in the area of moral philosophy.

Again, I don't want to claim that this *comes into ethics* with Kant; I think that the ideas of moral equality and universal moral concern are already present in the Jerusalem-based religions[10] (they are implicit in the idea that every human being is made in the image of God).[11] These ideas are also seen in Confucianism, for example in the endless concern of Confucius (and of other Chinese philosophers as well) with the problems (including unemployment, war, and poverty) of the humblest people, and the fact that Chinese thinkers seem to tell us both that anyone can be a sage and that no one is a sage.[12] (Similar examples can be given in Hinduism and Buddhism.) Nor was Kant the first to treat the idea of equality philosophically; as Martha Nussbaum has pointed out, one can find powerful formulations in ancient Stoicism.[13] But after Stoicism, with the increasing valorization of the Roman Empire (and later the monarchial nation-state), the idea of *universal* ethical equality was largely lost for more than a millennium, to reappear in the Enlightenment, and as an idea that stirred the whole age, in the French Revolution; and it was Kant who, above all, formulated the idea, the theme of universalism, in the most compelling way for his time, and for subsequent times as well.

Aristotle too was on my list. Although Aristotle was turned into a universalist (or "cosmopolitan") thinker by the Stoics and later philosophers, I myself do not find in Aristotle's *Nicomachean Ethics*, wonderful as that book is, a clear concern with universal community. Rather, Aristotle's ethics is concerned with the question, "What is the nature of the most admirable human life?" And while we do not need to agree with Book X of the *Nicomachean Ethics* that there is just *one* kind of human life that is most admirable, while we can recognize that there are many different forms of human flourishing, and at best a partial ordering of types of human flourishing, it still seems to me that the *Nicomachean Ethics* constitutes the classical meditation (in every sense of the word "classical") on the question, "What makes a human life admirable?" In particular, the great Aristotelian definition of human flourishing *(eudaimonia)* as "the activity of the psyche—the whole human mind and spirit—according to virtue in the complete life," I find as profound today as it must have been two-plus millennia ago.[14]

There are tensions between the concern of Levinasian ethics, which is situational in the extreme, and the concerns of Kant and Aristotle. Levinas's thought experiment is always to imagine myself confronted with *one* single suffering human being, ignoring for the moment the likelihood that I am already under obligation to many other human beings. I am supposed to feel the obligation to help *this* human being, an obligation which I am to experience not as the obligation to obey a *principle*, as a Kantian would, but as an obligation *to that human being*. Kant's concern, that I have at least one universal *principle*—the principle of always treating the humanity in another person as an end, and not merely as a means—a principle which I am not willing to allow to be overridden by considerations of utility, obviously pulls in a different direction, and both the Levinasian concern with the immediate recognition of the other and the Kantian concern with principle have been seen as being in conflict with the Aristotelian concern with human flourishing.

But that is not the way I see things. The tension is real, but so is the mutual support. Kantian ethics, I have argued[15] (as Hegel already argued) is, in fact, empty and formal unless we supply it with content precisely from Aristotelian and Levinasian and yet other directions. (Among those other directions, one might mention today concerns with democracy, concerns with toleration, concerns with pluralism, and, of course, still many others.) And Levinas is right to remind us that even if the ethical person acts in accordance with the Categorical Imperative, her focus is not on the Kantian principle as an abstract rule, but on the particular other person she is trying to help.

Most ethicists, however, down to the present day, still opt for one or another of the concerns I have listed, or perhaps opt simply for the Utilitarian concern with maximizing pleasure (the greatest pleasure of the greatest number for the longest period of time, or some successor to that formula) and try either to deny the ethical significance of the other concerns or else to reduce them to their favorite concern. It is as if they wanted to see ethics as a noble statue standing at the top of a single pillar.

My image is rather different. My image would be of a table with many legs. We all know that a table with many legs wobbles when the floor on which it stands is not even, but such a table is very hard to turn over, and that is how I see ethics: as a table with many legs, which wobbles a lot, but is very hard to turn over.

Practical Problems

At this point, I want to bring another philosopher, and not just another concern but a different conception altogether, into the picture, and that philosopher is John Dewey. Dewey has written on virtually all aspects of ethics, and on all the historic figures, and, like Kant (but unlike virtually all contemporary ethicists), has written a major work on aesthetics, but I shall focus on just one feature of his thought.[16] What I want to stress from Dewey is the idea of ethics as concerned with the solution of *practical* problems. But, given the caricatures of Pragmatism that one encounters, I must immediately say that "practical problems" here means simply "problems we encounter in practice," specific and situated problems, as opposed to abstract, idealized, or theoretical problems. "Practical" does not mean "instrumental," although instrumental thinking is *part* of what the solution of a practical problem typically involves. What is important is that practical problems, unlike the idealized thought experiments of the philosophers, are typically "messy." They do not have clear-cut solutions, but there are better and worse ways of approaching a given practical problem. One cannot normally expect to find a "scientific" solution to a practical problem, in the sense of "scientific" for which physics is the paradigm, and usually not even in the sense in which the statistical investigations in the social sciences are paradigmatic "scientific" investigations, although when the problems are large-scale social problems, social scientific investigations are certainly a necessary part of the investigation, as Dewey stressed. What I want to spend a moment on is the connection, to which I shall return in lecture 4, between the *controversiality* of many ethical views, and the fact that those views typically arise as responses to *practical* problems.

When I speak of "controversiality," I do not have in mind controversies provoked by questions of a sweeping skeptical nature, for instance, "Why should I care about suffering at all?" I do not believe that someone who stands outside the whole circle of related concerns I have described as constitutive of ethics can be brought to share any one of them by argument alone, and if such a one were brought to act ethically by the force of a *non-ethical* reason, although the conduct that resulted might be "ethical," the *person* would not have become an ethical person (not at that stage, anyway). Historically, I think that the "macho" ethics, the ethics of "courage and manly prowess" that I described earlier, was only superseded when large numbers of people began to see that someone who refused to play that game was not necessarily a "wimp." It was the great moral exemplars of the world—the Buddha, Moses, Confucius, Jesus, Socrates, and many others—who demonstrated *in life* that there could be *glory*—glory, and yes, *dignity*—in siding with the victims of plunder and conquest, with the poor and downtrodden, rather than with the heroic Roman general, or the Viking chieftain, or whatever. But the fact that there is no way of justifying standing within the ethical life from outside does not mean that reason and justification have no place *within* the ethical life. They are necessary within the ethical life for the obvious reason that people who share the concerns I described as constitutive of ethics still often find themselves in disagreement.

Some philosophers have suggested that the persistence of disagreement is, indeed, reason to think there is no truth or justification to be found in ethics (for some reason, they do not usually suggest that the persistence of disagreement in philosophy, including disagreement about *this very question,* means that philosophical views—of which their own view is an example—are neither true nor justified). And often they support this suggestion by painting a rosy picture of factual disagreement, in which *all* factual disagreements are said to be such that we can "converge" on a right answer, such that we can reach consensus. They give this rosy picture a shade of plausibility by providing examples of disagreements in exact science, theoretical disagreements about the explanation of reproducible phenomena. But—and this is the point I want to emphasize—it isn't just that *ethical* disagreements aren't like that, *practical* disagreements *in general* aren't like that, even when they are not ethical, or not obviously ethical. Putative solutions to practical problems are controversial (unless they are put in practice and succeed to the satisfaction of all those involved), for a whole series of reasons, some of which I shall discuss in lecture 4.

One last observation before I leave this topic: when a practical problem is successfully solved, there is still often controversy as to whether the successful solution can be generalized to *the next* problem that seems similar; for the degree and significance of the *similarity* are typically controversial as well! What Dewey concluded from all this, early and late, was the following:

1. The aim of philosophy in general, and ethics in particular, should not be *infallibility* (or a set of eternal theoretical truths). The philosopher who wrote that "Philosophy recovers itself when it ceases to be a device for dealing with the problems of philosophers and becomes a method, cultivated by philosophers, for dealing with the problems of men"[17] emphasized throughout his long life that philosophies arise out of time-bound reactions to specific problems faced by human beings in given cultural circumstances. If a philosopher can contribute to the reasoned resolution of some of the problems of his or her time, that is no small achievement, and that some of her assumptions will in the future no doubt have to be qualified or even rejected is only to be expected. Our task as philosophers isn't to achieve "immortality."

2. In particular, the ethical recommendations that Dewey himself made were either addressed to specific problems—especially to problems of democratic education—or, if they were general, they were *methodological.*[18] If we can improve the way we deal with specific evils, with the hunger and violence and inequality that mar our world, we need not be disappointed if we cannot distill out from our

dealings a textbook of universal ethical truths that
will infallibly guide all future generations.

Conclusion

In this opening lecture I have explained my terms, and I have
just laid out a conception of ethics as concerned with the solution of practical problems, guided by many mutually supporting but not fully reconcilable concerns. It is, I think,
clear that this conception is not one that lends itself to
inflationary or reductive nor yet to nominalistic ontologizing. That is not yet an argument that something is wrong
with the project of ontology as such; the ontologist, or some
ontologists anyway, may well retort: "So much the worse for
ethics." If I am to justify the title of my final lecture in Part I,
"Ontology: An Obituary," I must now leave the topic of ethics (I will be touching on it again in the third and fourth lectures, however), and turn to ontology, to an examination of
what we are doing when we say that various sorts of entities
"exist." I shall begin that examination in my next lecture, in
which I explain a doctrine I call "Conceptual Relativity." It
has evoked controversy, as the title of that lecture perhaps
indicates: "A *Defense* of Conceptual Relativity."

A Defense of Conceptual Relativity

In the previous lecture I painted a picture of our ethical life, and I suggested that that picture accords ill with the ambitions of ontologists of all the varieties that I listed. But now the time has come to exchange the broad brush with which I painted my picture for a set of much finer brushes, to provide, in short, a much more detailed case against Ontology (especially in its contemporary analytic version) before I pronounce my obituary on the subject at the end of Part I.

What I want to do here is describe in some detail two phenomena that ontologists have always had enormous difficulty in accommodating. I shall call them *conceptual relativity* and *conceptual pluralism*. (A third, which I shall not discuss in this volume,[1] but which ontologists also have great difficulty in acknowledging, is the familiar phenomenon of *vagueness*.) I begin with conceptual relativity.

Conceptual Relativity

One great philosopher who described at least a special case of the phenomenon of conceptual relativity was Kant. I am thinking of the Second Antinomy in the Dialectic of the *Critique of Pure Reason*, about which I shall say a word later. That "antinomy," or rather the part that will concern us, has to do with the question whether points are genuine individuals, of which space consists (in which case Kant said they would be "simples"), or whether they are "mere limits." (The question whether points are simples or mere limits, however, goes all the way back to the ancient Greek philosophers, most—perhaps all—of whom thought that an extended entity, such as a region, could not consist of "extensionless" entities, such as simple points would be.) But I want to begin with a much less familiar (though more easily surveyable) problem, the problem of the status of what are called "mereological sums."

The subject of "mereology" was founded by the Polish logician Lezniewski (1886–1939), who was in turn inspired by a remark of Husserl's. Husserl was aware that logicians think of sets (of what are sometimes called "classes") as entities that do not have a location in space. For example, although each strawberry has a location in space (and time), the class of all strawberries (or "the set of all strawberries," as logicians are apt to say nowadays) is not located *anywhere*. It is, as Quine taught philosophers to say, an "abstract entity." Similarly, the set of all counties in Massachusetts is an abstract entity. Each county in Massachusetts has a location, which is precisely shown on the map of Massachusetts, but the set of all counties in Massachusetts isn't shown on the map, because it isn't anywhere. The relation that each county in Massachusetts bears to the set of all the counties is the relation of *set membership*. The counties are not *parts* of that set; they *belong* to it, but they are not parts of it in the way that my hand is a part of my body. The relation of set membership is generally symbolized by the Greek letter "ϵ" (epsilon); Somerset County (one of the counties in Massachusetts) bears this relation to the set of counties in Massachusetts:

Somerset County ϵ *{x| x is a county in Massachusetts}*

The theory of sets and set membership was first developed (albeit in a way that was not free of paradoxes) by the great nineteenth-century mathematician Cantor, and in the twentieth century was developed into an important and successful mathematical theory, one associated with the names of Zermelo, Fraenkel, and von Neumann (as well as with the name of Quine, although Quine's set theory is not one that most mathematicians bother with). Already in Husserl's day there was a considerable amount of precisely formalized set theory. Husserl pointed out, however, that the relation of a whole object to its parts—and when I say "whole object," think of a "thing" in the most common sense of the word, say a car or a rabbit, in short a genuine "substance" in the old Aristotelian sense—needed to be studied and axiomatized, and had not, in fact, been so.[2]

Lezniewski took up this challenge and created a subject called mereology, from the Greek word *meros* (part). Mereology is "the calculus of parts and wholes." But at the very beginning Lezniewski made a profoundly significant decision. Husserl had made it clear that by a "thing" he meant something that had a certain kind of *unity*. No more than Aristotle was Husserl prepared to count just any arbitrary assemblage of things as a *thing*. A heap of junk, or a scrambled pile of books, papers, and whatnot of the kind one frequently finds on my own messy writing desk, is not a thing in Aristotle's sense of a substance *(ousia),* nor would it be a thing in Husserl's sense. Lezniewski, for the sake of getting a tidy theory, decided to entirely ignore this philosophical restriction, and not just to ignore it, but to count the "sum" (as one speaks of it in mereology) of *any* two things (which may themselves be "sums") as a further "thing." For example, the sum of my nose and the Eiffel Tower is regarded as a perfectly good object in mereology.

A way of seeing the difference between mereological sums, in Lezniewski's sense, and classes is to go back to the example of Massachusetts and its counties. The mereological sum of all the counties in that state is, of course, the whole state of Massachusetts. But the mereological sum of all the plots of land and state parks, etc., in Massachusetts is *also* the whole state of Massachusetts; that is to say that Massachusetts can be decomposed into parts in more than one way. Similarly, the odd "object" I mentioned a few moments ago, the mereological sum of my nose and the Eiffel Tower, can be decomposed into parts in different ways; that mereological sum is also, for example, the mereological sum of the left half of my nose and the left half of the Eiffel Tower and the right half of my nose and the right half of the Eiffel Tower. It can be decomposed into two parts or four parts or virtually any number of parts. But the *set of all counties in Massachusetts* is not the same set as the set consisting of all the plots of land plus the state parks (and other legally recognized pieces of land that are not composed of plots) in Massachusetts. Somerset County is not a plot of land, state park, etc., although it is the sum of many plots of land, state parks, etc., and thus Somerset County is not a member ("ϵ") of this latter set, although it belongs to the former set; so it cannot be that the sets are *identical* with the corresponding mereological sums. In fact, the mereological sums have very good spatial locations (their spatial location is precisely the spatial location of Massachusetts), whereas the two sets consisting of the elements of two different partitionings of Massachusetts have no spatial location.

In several of my writings (I must admit that I have come in for some sharp attacks because of this) I have taken the view that while we can indeed speak as Lezniewski taught us to speak—we can say that there are such things as mereological sums, we can tell which mereological sums are identical and which are not identical, we can say that mereological sums are not identical with sets, etc.—to ask whether mereological sums *really exist* would be stupid.[3] It is, in my view, a matter of *convention* whether we say that mereological sums exist or not.

But what does this mean? How can the question whether something *exists* be a matter of *convention?* The answer, I suggest, is this: what logicians call "the existential quantifier," the symbol "($\exists x$)," and its ordinary language counterparts, the expressions "there are," "there exist" and "there exists a," "some," etc., *do not have a single absolutely precise use but a whole family of uses.* These uses are not totally different; for example, in all of its uses the existential quantifier obeys the same logical laws, the law, for instance, that if we say that all things have a certain property, then we can infer that there is something which has that property[4] (in logical symbols: from "$(x)Fx$" we can infer "$(\exists x)Fx$"), and the law that if we say that there is something which is both F and G we can infer that there is something which is F and there is something which is G (in logical symbols: from "$(\exists x)(Fx \& Gx)$" we can infer "$(\exists x)Fx \& (\exists x)Gx$"). But these properties of the existential quantifier and the related properties of its close relative the universal quantifier "(x)" ("for all x") do not fully determine how we are to use these expressions. In particular, there is nothing in the logic of existential and universal quantification to *tell us* whether we should say that mereological sums exist or don't exist; nor is there some other science that answers this question. I suggest that we can *decide* to say either. We can, in short, create divergent uses of the existential quantifier itself, and, to some extent—as I will illustrate when we come shortly to the topic of *pluralism*—we have always invented new, and in some cases divergent, uses of existential quantification.

What difference will it make whether we decide to count mereological sums as objects or not? Well, for one thing, it will make a difference to how many *objects* we say there are in a particular universe of discourse. Here is an example:[5]

Consider a world with three individuals, x_1, x_2, x_3, which are not further decomposable within that universe of discourse—say three point particles, of which two have "spin up" and one has "spin down." I will suppose that Rudolf Carnap (who liked to imagine very small universes like this when he was studying inductive logic in the 1950s) would have described the world as I just have: as "a world with three individuals."[6]

Now, suppose that we add the calculus of parts and wholes invented by Lezniewski to our logical apparatus. Then (if we ignore the so-called "null object") we will find that the world of three individuals, as I just imagined Carnap describing it, actually contains seven objects, as shown in the table below.

World 1 (A world à la Carnap)	World 2 ("Same" world à la Lezniewski)
x_1, x_2, x_3	$x_1, x_2, x_3,$
	$x_1 + x_2, x_1 + x_3, x_2 + x_3,$
	$x_1 + x_2 + x_3$

In *The Many Faces of Realism*, I called the phenomenon I have been describing—the fact that in certain cases what exists may depend on which of various conventions we adopt—*conceptual relativity*. Not surprisingly, the attack that is most often directed against the very idea of such a phenomenon is a dilemma. My critics typically say, *"Well, either you are just talking about mere change of meaning, or what you are saying is unintelligible. After all, if 'exist' has the same meaning in 'There is an object which is the mereological sum of x_1, x_2, and x_3' and 'There does not exist such a thing as the mereological sum of x_1, x_2, and x_3,' when the first sentence is in Lezniewski's language and the second is in Carnap's language, then Carnap and Lezniewski simply contradict each other. If they don't simply contradict each other, then they are talking past each other, simply using the word 'exist' in different ways. In fact, what your hypothetical Carnap (who, of course, is not the real Carnap, who had no objection to mereology) means by 'there exists' is 'there exists something which is not a mereological sum.' In other words, 'Carnap' is simply quantifying over a restricted universe of discourse; since he has left mereological sums out of his universe of discourse,*

*then of course in his sense of 'exist' it is true that there don't ex-
ist any mereological sums, and, in fact, since he has included as
individuals in his universe of discourse only x_1, x_2, and x_3, it is
true that, as he uses the words 'individual' and 'exist' there exist only three individuals (not counting sets or other abstract
entities as individuals) in this universe of discourse; while, as
Lezniewski, who has decided on a more inclusive universe of
discourse, uses 'exist,' there do exist seven individuals in his
universe of discourse. Your 'conceptual relativity' is merely an
example of the possibility of using 'exist' in a more inclusive or
a less inclusive way."*

I want to come back to this criticism and examine it in detail shortly. Note, by the way, that this criticism, taken at face
value, assumes that of course there *are* such things as
mereological sums, and the *only* question as to what "exists"
means here is whether to count *them* as individuals or not to
count *them* as individuals (i.e., as non-abstract objects).

"Difference of Meaning"

First I want to say a word about the notion "difference of
meaning." The word "meaning" and its relatives may be used
in a sense closely connected with linguistics (counting lexi-
cography as part of linguistics). Using the notion in this way,
we ask what a word means, and expect to be given, if not a
synonym, at least a paraphrase of a kind that any native
speaker of the relevant language might give, or if the paraphrase is in a different language, one that counts as a reasonable translation. This is the notion of meaning that concerns
Donald Davidson, my predecessor in the Hermes Lectures.
In this sense of "meaning," the criterion as to whether two

expressions have the same meaning is translation practice. But there is another, perhaps looser, notion of meaning made famous by Wittgenstein, in which to ask for the meaning of a word is to ask how it is used, and explanations of how a word is used may often involve technical knowledge of a kind ordinary speakers do not possess, and may be of a kind that would never appear in a lexicon or be offered as translations. In short, there is a difference between *elucidating* the meaning of an expression by describing how it is used, and giving its meaning in the Davidsonian, or narrow linguistic, sense.

I agree that in this looser, Wittgensteinian sense of meaning, meaning as use, the user of Lezniewski's language (henceforth "the Polish Logician") and my imaginary Carnap are giving different meanings, that is, different *uses*, to "exist" in the context described. What I deny is that the difference *must* be described in a way that begs the question as to the existence of mereological sums, that is, has to be described by saying that the Polish Logician *includes* mereological sums in his or her universe of discourse. There is a description of the Polish Logician's use of "exist" which does not make the assumption that there *are* mereological sums to be "included" or "not included" in one's universe of discourse (in Quine's language, a description in a metalanguage which does not include mereological sums in its "ontology," although it does include *sets* in its ontology). Here is the description: the Polish Logician speaks as if, corresponding to any set of (more than one) individuals in a "Carnapian" universe, there is a further individual which has as parts the members of that set.[7] As a spatial location, the Polish Logician assigns to this supposed (or pretended) individual the spatial region which is the geometrical sum of the regions (which may be points) occupied by the Carnapian individuals in the set. *This* description is neutral as to whether these supposed or pretended individuals are "real" individuals or mere logical constructions.[8]

The explanation I just gave as to how the Polish Logician uses her language is not a *translation* of the words "exist" and "object" as used by the Polish Logician. It is not part of a Davidsonian "meaning theory" of the Polish Logician's language; it is, rather, a *manual of instructions* for talking the way the Polish Logician talks. But it describes the difference between the way the Polish Logician *uses* her language and the way the Carnapian logician *uses* her language. In the wide sense of the term "meaning," meaning as use, there is a difference in "meaning" here. But it is not *trivial,* because it is not the case that the person who gives this description of the Polish Logician's language has to agree that what the Polish Logician says is *true,* or that the disagreement between the Carnapian logician and the Polish Logician is "only apparent." The neutral description allows for the possibility that someone might think that there *aren't* any such things as "mereological sums,"[9] that the whole idea of "mereological sums" is crazy. Such a person might say, "Well look; what the Polish Logician says is *literally* false, but I 'understand' it in the sense that I can *reinterpret* what the Polish Logician says so that it comes out true. Mereology, so reinterpreted, is just a convenient fiction; the pretense that there is such an object as the sum of my nose and the Eiffel Tower is just a convenient fiction."

What I call "conceptual relativity" is not the mere recognition that there are cases of this kind. After all, one might recognize that there are cases of this kind and do something analogous to what Kant did in the Second Antinomy; one might say that the question "Do mereological sums really exist?" is an antinomy, that the mind (which is allegedly unable to get down to "things as they are in themselves") can't *know* whether mereological sums really exist or do not, or even know whether the question is appropriately conceived or not, and must tangle itself in contradictions if it tries to answer it.[10] That attitude is not the attitude that I am calling "conceptual relativity." Conceptual relativity, as I already indicated, holds that the question as to which of these ways of using "exist" (and "individual," "object," etc.) is *right* is one that the meanings of the words in the natural language, that is, the language that we all speak and cannot avoid speaking every day, simply leaves open. Both the set theory that developed in the nineteenth (and early twentieth) century and the mereology that Lezniewski invented are what I will call *optional languages* (a term suggested by Jennifer Case),[11] in the sense that one may count as a master of the (English or German or Polish . . .) language without learning these particular sublanguages. The optional language of set theory and the optional language of mereology represent possible *extensions* of our ordinary ways of speaking. If we adopt mereology, or if we adopt both mereology and set theory, then of course we will say that there exist mereological sums. If we adopt set theory but reject mereology as unnecessary or useless, then we will say that mereological sums do not exist, although, of course, one can use the language of mereology as a *façon de parler* if one wishes.[12] But the question whether mereological sums "really exist" is a silly question. It is *literally* a matter of convention whether we decide to say they exist.

But didn't Quine destroy the notion of "truth by convention"? Well, he certainly destroyed the idea that the laws of logic are, one and all, true by convention.[13] But I am not urging that the laws of logic are true by convention. And he correctly saw that, while there is an element of convention in all knowledge, there is no guarantee that anything we call a convention won't someday have to be given up, perhaps for a reason we are totally unable to foresee now. But I am not claiming that conventions of the kind I am describing might never have to be given up for presently unforeseeable reasons. That would be a crazy claim. There is a perfectly good sense of convention, as David Lewis pointed out long ago in a book with that very title,[14] in which a convention is simply a *solution to a certain kind of coordination problem.* Driving on the left side of the road is the solution to a coordination problem adopted in the United Kingdom, Australia, and in Eire, and driving on the right is the solution to the same coordination problem adopted in all or most of the rest of the world. It is *literally* a "matter of convention" which side one drives on. And no metaphysics of "analyticity" or "apriority" or "unrevisability" is involved in saying this. In the same sense of convention, I claim, it is a matter of convention whether one decides, in a given formal context, to accept the axioms of mereology.

Quine ended a famous paper[15] in which he criticized the idea that some sentences are true by convention by describing "the lore of our fathers" as a gray fabric—"black with fact and white with convention." And he added, "but I have not found any quite black threads nor any wholly white ones."

The problem with Quine's formulation is that to speak of two components (two "colors," white and black) in this way suggests that we should be able to analyze our knowledge as a chemist analyzes a compound—able, that is, to say *how much* white dye and how much black dye any given "thread" is covered with. But to do this would be precisely to revert to the idea of facts about the world as it is apart from all convention, for that is what a description of the "black dye," a statable factual component, unadulterated with any "white dye" would amount to.

As I once suggested,[16] a better way to describe the situation would be to say that our empirical knowledge, or any piece of it, is conventional relative to certain alternatives and factual relative to certain others. Saying that there are three objects in the universe of discourse Carnap was describing is a matter of fact, as opposed to saying that there are four objects in that universe, and a matter of convention, as opposed to describing the situation in Lezniewski's language by saying that there are seven objects (counting the mereological sums as objects). Of course, my critics would not challenge this. But they fail to see that the convention in question doesn't have to be described in a way that assumes that of course one grants the "existence" of mereological sums. It can simply be described as a choice between two specifiable ways of using words.

Do Carnap and Lezniewski "Contradict" Each Other?

I have now discussed the senses in which Carnap and Lezniewski do, and in which they do not, give the words "exist" and "object" different *meanings.* Let me now say a word about the sense in which Carnap and Lezniewski do and do not "contradict" each other.

The example of conceptual relativity so far mentioned, as well as the example I shall discuss next and the more technical examples from physics I have used in some of my papers,[17] all involve statements that *appear* to be contradictory (if we simply conjoin them, ignoring the different uses that they have in their respective optional languages, we get a contradiction), but *are not in fact contradictory,* if we understand each of them as belonging to a different optional language, and recognize that the two optional languages involve the choices of incompatible conventions. What are "incompatible" are not the statements themselves, which cannot simply be conjoined, but the conventions.

The way in which I would treat the example from Kant's Second Antinomy is, of course, exactly the way in which I just treated the "question" of the "existence" of mereological sums. We can formalize geometry by taking points as primitive, and defining regions to be sets of points (this is one *optional language*), and we can formalize geometry by taking regions as primitive and taking points to be sets of convergent regions (this is a different *optional language*). To ask which is "really correct" is silly. All the statements we care about in geometry are independent of the choice of one or another of these optional languages as our formalization of geometry. Nor is there some supernal fact as to whether points are "really" individuals that we can't know. Points are not entities we are causally connected with; if one point were removed from space, no physical process, not even the value of the gravitational or any other field at any other point, or the ψ-function at any given point in quantum field theory, would be changed even infinitesimally. All causal explanations are unaffected by the choice between these formalizations. There is no fact here *to be* known—not even by God. To suppose that "points are really individuals" has an unknowable truth value would be to suppose that "individual" has its meaning somehow fixed apart from its use, counting all the causal facts there are about the contexts in which we use it as part of its "use." But there is nothing that dictates a sublime "right sense" upon words like "individual," "object," "exist" in *that* way. Rather than regarding the "question" as an *antinomy*, as Kant did, we should, as we did in the mereological sums case, see the choice between these optional languages as a matter of *convention*.

Identity Statements and Conceptual Relativity

Nevertheless, a new element appears in this last case. What we see here is that certain *identity statements* exhibit the same phenomenon that we saw certain *existence statements* exhibit. For certain identity statements are left open by the meanings (i.e., the uses) of the words in ordinary language, and there are equally good choices as to how the openness is to be closed (if we want to close it, say for purposes of formalization). And these "equally good choices" give rise to a coordination problem whose solution is, again, a convention. Adopt one convention and $X = Y$ is true, where X is a certain point in space and Y is a certain set of regions, and adopt a different convention and it becomes false. But this is not a "difference in the meaning" of *point* in the Davidsonian (or lexicographer's) sense—because it neither creates any new nor changes any old synonymies—although it is a difference in the *use* of the word "point."

Conceptual Pluralism

In *Representation and Reality* I counted the fact that we might describe "the contents" of a room very differently by using first the vocabulary of fundamental physical theory and then again the vocabulary of tables and chairs and lamps and so on as a further instance of conceptual relativity, and this, I now think, was a mistake, although it *is* an instance of a related and wider phenomenon I should have called *conceptual pluralism*.[18] The fact that the contents of a room may be partly described in two very different vocabularies cannot be an instance of conceptual relativity in the sense just explained, because conceptual relativity always involves descriptions which are cognitively equivalent (in the sense that any phenomenon whose explanation can be given in one of the optional languages involved has a corresponding explanation in the other),[19] but which are incompatible if taken at face value (the descriptions cannot be simply conjoined). But the fact that the contents of a room may be partly described in the terminology of fields and particles and the fact that it may be partly described by saying that there is a chair in front of a desk are not in any way "incompatible," not even "at face value": the statements "the room may be partly described by saying there is a chair in front of a desk" and "the room may be partly described as consisting of fields and particles" don't even *sound* "incompatible." And they are not cognitively equivalent (even if we do not bar the fantastic possibility of defining terms like "desk" and "table" in the language of fundamental physics,[20] the field-particle description contains a great deal of information that is not translatable into the language of desks and chairs). That we

can use both of these schemes without being required to reduce one or both of them to some single fundamental and
universal ontology is the doctrine of pluralism; and while
conceptual relativity implies pluralism, the reverse is not the
case.

There is, however, a further connection between the pluralism characteristic of natural languages and the issues
raised by my examples of conceptual relativity. For while the
"ontology" of a given natural language, ignoring the optional sublanguages that we sometimes add to it, is for the
most part obligatory for speakers of that language, and while
virtually all natural languages have terms for tables and
chairs, etc.,[21] certain natural languages do sometimes quantify over "objects" which are unique to those languages. In
this way, they illustrate the possibility which we have seen to
be demonstrated by conceptual relativity, the possibility of
different *extensions* of our ordinary notions of *object* and *existence.*

Excellent examples of this occur in Benjamin Lee Whorf's
writings.[22] One runs as follows: the Shawnee, Whorf tells us,
utter two very similar sentences, morphologically and gram-
matically, when they say what we would express in English
by saying

(1)   *I have an extra toe on my foot.*

and

(2)   *I pull the branch aside.*

The morpheme-by-morpheme translation that Whorf
gives shows why and how such different assertions (from

our point of view) are able to be morphologically similar in Shawnee: there is a morpheme (l_i-thawa) in Shawnee that Whorf translates as "fork-tree" (i.e., "fork-shaped pattern"), and in Shawnee, the structure of (1) is:

(3)   *I fork-tree on-toes (have).*

while the structure of (4) is:

(4)   *I fork-tree by-hand-cause.*

Davidson has famously argued against Whorf that the very fact that Whorf could translate Shawnee into English at all shows that there is no difference in "conceptual scheme" between the two languages, and the same argument is commonplace today in papers and courses on psycholinguistics.[23] However, this argument assumes that English already had *that* notion of a "fork-shaped pattern" (or "fork-tree") *before* Whorf wrote his paper. In fact, the whole argument of Davidson's "The Very Idea of a Conceptual Scheme" assumes that *translation leaves the language into which we translate unaffected.* I deny both of these premises. I think Shawnee has an "ontology" of patterns that (normal) English lacks, although we could, of course, *add* it to English; and I think that the conceptual scheme of English is constantly being enriched by interactions with other languages, as well as by scientific, artistic, etc., creations.

But we do not need to confine ourselves to exotic languages. The English word "mind" is notoriously untranslatable into other European languages (unless they just *decide* to let *esprit* or *Geist* have the sense of the English "mind"). In fact, philosophy lecturers often use the English word rather

than any local word. We have "minds" in our English ontology, and minds are not quite the same as *esprits* or *Geister,* or
as Hebrew *ruchot,* etc. The French recognize a phenomenon
they call *nonchalance,* and we have simply borrowed the
word into English, precisely because we *didn't* have a good
translation in English. "Quantifying over" various patterns
is not optional for a Shawnee; "quantifying over" minds is
not optional for an English speaker; and so forth. But although English, Shawnee, French, etc., are not "optional languages," the whole collection of human languages now in
existence illustrates how many ways there are of "quantifying" in the process of describing very simple situations, situations as simple as someone's pulling a branch aside. The
whole idea that the *world* dictates a unique "true" way of di-
viding the world into objects, situations, properties, etc., is a
piece of philosophical parochialism. But just that parochialism is and always has been behind the subject called
Ontology.

But there is something else wrong with Ontology, and
that is the idea that each and every instance of objectivity
must be supported by *objects.* This remark sounds puzzling,
I know. How can there possibly be objectivity without objects? That will be the subject of my next lecture.

Objectivity without Objects

As it is very often interpreted, Plato's theory of Ideas represents an early appearance of two persistent philosophical ideas: the idea that if a claim is objectively true, then there have to be *objects* to which the claim "corresponds"—an idea which is built into the very etymology of the word "objective"—and the corollary idea that if there are no obvious natural objects whose properties would make the claim true, then there must be some *non-natural* objects to play the role of "truth-maker." As we saw, the same two ideas (plus some confusions of his own)[1] figure in G. E. Moore's idea that if there are truths as to the goodness of certain states of affairs, then there must be a "non-natural property" *"good,"* to account for this. Accept these two ideas, and you are likely to accept a third, the idea that if a claim is true, then the claim is a *description* of whatever objects and properties make it true.

Accept all three ideas, and, if you regard some value judgments as objectively true, you will conclude that they are *descriptions;* and if you cannot construe them to your own satisfaction as descriptions of natural objects and properties, you will be forced to construe them as descriptions which refer to non-natural entities. It is this very understandable, but I believe totally mistaken, line of thought that I will be concerned to criticize in both this lecture and the final one. Here, however, I shall not deal with the topic of ethical values, except for these opening remarks.

Incidentally, it is not only philosophers like the "Plato" of the tradition or G. E. Moore who assume that all objectively true statements are descriptions of reality. In a fine paper discussing this issue,[2] James Conant pointed out that two philosophers sympathetic to Wittgenstein's views (as they variously interpret them), Sabina Lovibond and Simon Blackburn, have attributed to Wittgenstein forms of the view I am going to criticize. Lovibond, for example, wrote that "Wittgenstein's view of language implicitly denies any metaphysical role to the idea of reality; it denies that we can draw any principled distinction between those parts of assertoric discourse which do, and those which do not, genuinely *describe* reality."[3] She concluded that for Wittgenstein, *all* genuine assertions, including ethical and mathematical ones, can be said to "describe reality." To quote her exact words: "The only way, then, in which an indicative statement can fail to describe reality is by *not being true*— i.e., by virtue of reality not being as the statement declares it to be."[4]

Blackburn's response was that one cannot take this interpretation seriously as a reading of Wittgenstein, on the following grounds:

(1) "Wittgenstein constantly wants to force the *difference* between different language games right down our throats";[5] and

(2)   "He is constantly suggesting that underneath a
        superficial similarity in linguistic form there is a
        deep difference in function."[6]

Blackburn thinks (correctly in my opinion) that Wittgenstein would *not* agree that the function of *all* ethical and
mathematical sentences is to "describe reality." But what
Blackburn concludes from this is that Wittgenstein must
be some sort of antirealist about ethical and mathematical
assertions.

Describing how I would react to this dispute, Conant
writes that

> To the extent that Wittgenstein does indeed hold to his two
> basic principles [(1) and (2)], Putnam will want to side with
> Blackburn. But there is something in Lovibond's "realism"
> which Putnam wants, nevertheless, to try to hang on to—the
> idea that ethical and mathematical propositions are *bona fide*
> instances of assertoric discourse: ethical and mathematical
> thought represents forms of reflection that are as fully gov-
> erned by norms of truth and validity as any other form of
> cognitive activity. But he is not friendly to the idea that, in or-
> der to safeguard the cognitive credentials of ethics and math-
> ematics, one must therefore suppose that ethical and mathe-
> matical talk bear on reality *in the same way* as ordinary
> empirical thought, so that in order to safeguard the truth of
> such propositions as "it is wrong to break a promise" or
> "2 + 2 = 4," one must suppose that, like ordinary empirical
> propositions, such propositions, in each sort of case, 'de-
> scribe' their own peculiar states of affairs. There is an as-
> sumption at work here that Putnam wants to reject—one
> which underlies Blackburn's way of distinguishing realism
> and antirealism—the assumption that there are just two ways
> to go: either (i) we accept a general philosophical account of

the relation between language and reality according to which all indicative sentences are to be classified equally as 'descriptions of reality'; or (ii) we accept an alternative account of the relation between language and reality which rests on a metaphysically-grounded distinction between those sentences which do genuinely describe reality (and whose cognitive credentials are therefore to be taken at face value) and those which merely purport to describe reality (and whose claims to truth are therefore to be taken as chimerical).[7]

Conant has described very succinctly just the views that I want to argue for here. The paper of mine that he was referring to was a lecture to the Aristotelian Society about the later Wittgenstein's philosophy of mathematics,[8] one which was itself an abridgment of a much longer paper that has since appeared,[9] but I shall be less technical than I was in that longer paper.

Objectivity without Objects: The Case of Logic

"Still," one may wonder, "how can there be such a thing as a *truth* which is not a description of some object or objects?" Actually, however, examples of statements which are uncontroversially true, but which cannot without metaphysical fantasy be understood as descriptions of objects, are not hard to give. Perhaps the most obvious examples are statements from logic. Consider, for example, a statement that *explicitly* talks about logical connection, that is, about what is a *consequence* of what, what *follows from* what—for example, the following statement:

If all platypuses are egg-laying mammals, then *it follows that* anything that is not an egg-laying mammal is not a platypus.

True, you can call this a description, if you like—you might say it's a description of "the logical relation between two statements," the statement that all platypuses are egg-laying mammals and the statement that anything that is not an egg-laying mammal is not a platypus; but few philosophers today think it right to take talk of "describing relations between statements" with inflationary metaphysical earnestness, that is, to think that we are literally *describing* a certain sort of *relation* between certain *intangible objects* when we point out the validity of a simple logical inference in this way.[10] To think that is to be a "Platonist" in one's philosophy of logic. And when I say that we are not describing "objects" when we say that an inference is valid, or, to change the example, when we say that a statement is a "tautology," I want to make it clear that it is "Platonism" that I am attacking, and not the propriety of using the word "description" in connection with remarks such as "that is a valid inference" or "that is a tautology."

An objection to what I have just said that I am sure will occur to some of my readers is that one can think of inferences and statements as objects without being in any way a "Platonist." In mathematical logic we sometimes do identify statements with sequences of *marks*,[11] and we define a mathematical property of these sequences that we call "validity" in a purely set-theoretic way. I shall shortly argue that it is a mistake to take talk of "set-theoretic objects" with full (i.e., inflationary) metaphysical earnestness, that is, to think that we are literally *describing* a realm of "intangible objects" when we do set theory. But even if we think that there is, there is no sense in which a *sentence* (in the sense in which formal model theory speaks of sentences, that is, as mere sequences of marks) *can* "follow from" another sentence, or have another sequence of marks as a "consequence," or in which a mere sequence of marks can be "valid." The standard way of treating "validity" in mathematical logic is a way of *doing without* the notion, not a way of analyzing it.

To illustrate the claim I just made so briefly and dogmatically, let us consider the approach of Quine in his *Methods of Logic*. Quine defined a "tautology" (i.e., a logical truth in propositional calculus) to be *an instance of a schema all of whose substitution instances are true.* (As an example, think of the schema "$p \supset p \lor q$".)[12] But this Quinian definition is unsatisfactory for several reasons.

(1) Quine's definition applies only to sentences in an artificial language. There are (as I am sure Quine would agree) no schemas—that is, fixed grammatical forms—all of whose instances in a *natural language* are true.

(2) As soon as we restrict his definition—as Quine certainly intended—to a formalized language for which a Tarskian truth-definition can be given, we have failed to capture what may be called the *universality* of logical truth. To say that all instances of, for example, "$p \supset p \lor q$" *in a particular vocabulary* are true isn't the same thing as saying that those instances (e.g., "If every swan in the Kinneret is white, then every swan in the Kinneret is white or every swan in the Kinneret is overweight") are *logically true*—it is to say much less.

One reason that the truth of all substitution instances in a particular language is, conceptually speaking, much less than logical validity has to do with what Tarski actually did and did not accomplish with his "definitions of truth." Something which is still often missed to this day is that Tarski did not even attempt to define "true in L" for *variable* L, that is, to define truth in *general.* What he showed is how, *given a fixed language* L—*given one particular formally regimented language,* to define a predicate that is *coextensive* with the property of being a true sentence in that language.[13]

In fact, "true-in-L" (as defined by a Tarskian "truth definition") is an expression whose *definiens* contains *no* occurrences of the name "L". The word "L", which elsewhere designates a particular language, occurs only *accidentally* in the expression "true-in-L", just as "cat" occurs only accidentally in "cattle."[14] And since a Tarskian "truth definition" provides no *general* notion of truth, but only an infinite series of different notions, "true-in-L_1", true-in- L_2",..., then Quine's definition of validity, presupposing, as it does, that Tarski *has* provided a purely extensional explanation of the predicate "true," likewise provides only an infinite series of different notions of validity, "valid-in-L_1", "valid-in-L_2", etc., and not a single notion "valid" applicable (truly or falsely, but in any case meaningfully) to statements in an arbitrary language.

(3) Moreover, Quine's definition of truth-functional validity as "truth of all substitution instances"—that is, truth-in-L of all substitution instances—is not extensionally correct in all cases. Consider, for example, a language L_E whose logical connectives are just ∧, ∨, and ⊃, and whose atomic sentences—suppose these include "The Eiffel Tower is in Paris" and "Seattle is in Washington State"—all happen to be true. Every substitution instance of the schema "$q \supset p$" is true in L_E, but "If the Eiffel Tower is in Paris then Seattle is in Washington State" is not a tautology!

(4) A final problem with the Quinian definition of logical truth is that to say that a statement, be it in an artificial nota-

tion or in natural language, is logically true (or is a "tautology") is not just to say that it and some bunch of other sentences are all true, but that they are *necessarily* true, and this element—the *necessity* of logical truth is (of course, deliberately) left out of the Quinian account.

It might be objected that even if Quine did not succeed in explicating the intuitive notion of validity, still, "Isn't the sentence you used as an example, the sentence *If every swan in the Kinneret is white, then every swan in the Kinneret is white or every swan in the Kinneret is overweight,* a description of the swans in the Kinneret?" Aren't valid sentences made true by objects the way their constituents are? But, as philosophers and logicians have always been aware, that is not a helpful way of looking at such a sentence, for this statement would still be true even if it turned out that we were mistaken in supposing that swans exist and that swans can be white and that the Kinneret exists. It is not the characteristics of swans that make the inference from "Every swan in the Kinneret is white" to "Every swan in the Kinneret is white or every swan in the Kinneret is overweight" correct, or the characteristics of reptiles and mammals that make "If all reptiles are mammals, then anything that is not a mammal is not a reptile" true. There are standards that logically valid inferences have to meet, and that logically true statements have to meet, and the inference in question and the statement in question do meet these respective standards. But those are not the standards that apply to what we ordinarily call "descriptions," e.g., "There are some cars parked next to the church." Logic is neither a description of nonnatural relations between transcendent "objects" nor a description of ordinary empirical properties of empirical objects.

There is no better example of what Wittgenstein cuttingly calls "the philosopher's *must*" than the idea that if a statement is true then it *must* be a description of some part of reality. The idea that there is a realm of intangible objects called "statements" (or maybe something called "the logical structure of the world"), and that a statement of logical consequence is a *description* of an intangible object or set of objects, is utterly empty as explanation. It fits all the criteria for what philosophers of science—and not only positivists, by the way—have long called a *pseudo-explanation*, namely:

(i)   It posits something we have found no other need to posit (and which is not, of course, observable by the senses—otherwise it wouldn't be a posit);

(ii) It does no work for us, because we derive nothing from it but the very phenomenon we posited it to explain (it lacks "surplus meaning")—this also makes it unfalsifiable, of course; and

(iii) Those who defend it do not suggest any way of extending it so that it *will* have surplus meaning— in short, it lacks fruitfulness *ab initio.*

Conceptual Truth

"But how do we know that statements of logic are correct if they are not descriptions of some part of reality?" Well, *some* statements, in fact the axioms of quantificational logic, are what I have elsewhere defended calling *conceptual truths.*[15] I am aware that, after Quine's attack on the analytic-synthetic distinction, the very idea of conceptual truth came itself to seem metaphysical. And it *becomes* metaphysical if one supposes, as Quine *and* his opponents did, that *which* truths are conceptual truths is something that we can know *incorrigibly*. The only sort of conceptual truth they recognized was analytic truth, and analytic truths were supposed to be an example of *unrevisable* knowledge, both by Quine and by his opponent-of-choice, Rudolf Carnap.[16] But there is an older view, one represented by both Hegelians and pragmatists at the beginning of the twentieth century, according to which conceptual truths are not "analytic" in the way that "All bachelors are unmarried" is thought to be analytic—they are not "trifling" truths, nor are they unrevisable. According to this tradition, we know that something is a conceptual truth by way of *interpretation*, and interpretation is itself an essentially corrigible activity.[17] Separate the idea of conceptual truth from the idea of unrevisable truth (and from the idea of truth by mere stipulation), and not one of Quine's arguments any longer has any force, especially if (as I think one must) one also gives up the idea that *every* truth can be classified as either a conceptual truth *or* a description of fact.

What makes a truth a conceptual truth, as I am using the term, is that it is impossible to make (relevant) sense of the *assertion* of its negation. This way of understanding the notion of conceptual truth fits well with the recognition that conceptual truth and empirical description interpenetrate; for when we say that the denial of a certain statement makes no sense, we always speak within the body of beliefs and concepts and conceptual connections that we accept, and it has sometimes happened that a scientific revolution overthrows enough of those background beliefs that *we come to see how* something that previously made no sense *could* be true. A by now familiar example is the discovery that there can actually exist triangles whose angles add up to more than two right angles.[18] Imagine that in 1700 someone had said, "There is a triangle whose angles add up to more than two right angles." Would these words have been intelligible? At best this would have been taken to be a riddle. We would doubtless have said, "I give up. What's the answer?" And if the speaker could say no more than, "I just mean that there is a triangle whose angles add up to more than 180°", then he would have been *literally* unintelligible. In 1700, he would have been speaking gibberish.

But as we all know, in the early decades of the nineteenth century Riemann discovered a "non-Euclidean" geometry in which the propositions "the sum of the angles in *any* triangle is always *greater* than two right angles" and "space is finite but unbounded" both hold true. And in 1916, the application of non-Euclidean geometry to physical space was elaborated into a highly successful physical theory by Einstein in his General Theory of Relativity. "There is a triangle whose angles add up to more than two right angles" is a statement that is *now* fully intelligible—intelligible because a huge body of background theory has changed.

The conception of conceptual truth that I defend, I repeat, recognizes the interpenetration of conceptual relations and facts, and it grants that there is an important sense in which knowledge of conceptual truth is corrigible. But, unlike Quine's conception, which scraps almost all distinctions among scientific truths (except for recognizing a small class of what Quine called "stimulus analytic" truths),[19] my conception regards it as a fact of great *methodological* (and not merely "psychological") significance, a matter of how inquiry is structured, that there are assertions whose negations *make no sense* if taken as serious assertions. For example, it *makes no sense* to say (*now,* with *our* conceptual resources), "All duck-billed platypuses are egg-laying mammals, but it is not true that everything that isn't an egg-laying mammal isn't a platypus." And this is of methodological—as opposed to purely "psychological"—significance[20] because the questions "How do you know that not-*p* isn't the case?" and "What *evidence* do you have that not-*p* isn't the case?" and "What *proof* do you have that not-*p* isn't the case?" are questions that can be raised and discussed only *if* we have succeeded in *making sense* of the "possibility that not-*p*." Conceptual truths are not "foundations of our knowledge" in the old absolute sense, but they are foundations in the sense that Wittgenstein pointed to when he wrote in *On Certainty* that "one might say these foundation walls are held up by the whole house."[21]

The Limits of Conceptual Truth as an Explanation

It would be an error, however, to think: "Oh, now we have accounted for the nature of logical truth; all logical truths are conceptual truths." In fact, logical truths are not all conceptual truths in the sense just described, the sense in which "2 + 2 = 4" and "If all platypuses are egg-laying mammals, then *it follows that* anything that is not an egg-laying mammal is not a platypus" are conceptual truths. It makes no sense to suppose that these statements are false (although, I repeat, in saying that, I am not claiming to have any sort of non-empirical guarantee that we will not one day perceive such a sense). But there are logical truths—truths of fairly elementary parts of logic, at that—that do not *seem* to be logical truths and that can only be *seen* to be logical truths by means of a *proof.* (This is even more conspicuously the case with mathematical truths.) In such cases, one may have the experience (which Wittgenstein often refers to in his *Remarks on the Foundations of Mathematics*) of *changing one's mind about whether one can conceive something.* That is, when confronted with something which turns out to be a contradiction, but which is not easily seen to be a contradiction, one may feel that one knows perfectly well what it would be for it to be true, and yet after one has seen the proof that it is a contradiction, not only will one say "Now I see that it couldn't be true," but it will seem that what one was doing when one thought one was "imagining that it was true" was not really *conceiving of a situation in which it would be true,* but doing something else. To know what it is for something to be a logical truth (in a sophisticated sense of the term), it is not enough to be familiar with a few examples of self-evident logical truth, such as the statement about platypuses above, but one must have some familiarity with *logical justification,* with the process of showing that a complex statement, or set of statements, which is not contradictory on its face, is really contradictory, or showing that a statement which is not, on its face, a logically necessary truth *is* a logically necessary truth. In short, one learns what logical truth *is* by learning the procedures and standards of logic. But nothing in those procedures and standards involves comparing the statements that one is trying to evaluate for logical truth (or logical consistency, or implication, etc.) with non-natural entities, such as the "propositions" that were dear to the hearts of British philosophers early in the twentieth century, or with "the logical structure of the world," to see whether they do or do not *describe* this mysterious part of reality.

Mathematical Truth

I began with this case, the case of logic, because logic is a subject that deals *par excellence* with the evaluation of reasons, with the forms of inferences and the forms of assertions, and with the evaluation of inferences as good or bad; and if there is anything that today's "naturalist" (in the sense of *scientistic*) metaphysicians tend to overlook, it seems to me, it is that judgments to the effect that such-and-such is a good reason are not *descriptions*. In the next lecture I shall come to the much more complicated case of ethical truths, but here I want to briefly say something about two other kinds of truths, namely *mathematical truths* and what I shall call *methodological value judgments* (I will explain shortly what I mean by the latter term).

In a sense, what I want to say about mathematical truth has already been indicated, but there is a complication to be noted, which is that whereas all truths of at least the elementary logic of quantifiers, so-called "quantification theory," are *provable*, there are good reasons, which I won't rehearse here, for believing that provability in pure mathematics is not coextensive with truth. I have in mind, of course, the Gödel Incompleteness Theorems, but not only these formal metamathematical results. These theorems do not, by themselves, tell us whether we should say of sentences in mathematics that can neither be proved nor disproved (Gödel's theorems showed that there are such sentences) that they can be true or false. But, as I have argued elsewhere,[22] none of the philosophies that try to identify mathematical truth with provability—whether "provability" is taken as a purely mathematical notion or is taken in some more "realistic" sense, say, as provability by actual human beings—none of these "finitist," or "intuitionist," or "quasi-realist"[23] philosophies of mathematics accords at all with the actual application of mathematics in physics. In particular, if one is unwilling, as I am, to be any sort of "instrumentalist" about physics, then the attempt to be an antirealist about mathematics while trying to be a realist in any sense about physics will run into fatal trouble. But to explain this any further would lead me into technical philosophy of mathematics and physics which is beyond the province of this volume.

Nevertheless, I think we can say with respect to mathematical truth what I just said about logical truth—that we learn what mathematical truth is by learning the practices and standards of mathematics itself, including the practices of *applying* mathematics. I would further add that to suppose that mathematical truths are "made true" by some set of *objects* runs into enormous troubles. First of all, the "objects" do not have clear identity relations. We are free in this area to stipulate in a surprising number of cases what the cross-category identity relations are: whether functions are a kind of set, or sets are a kind of function;[24] whether numbers are sets or not, and if they are sets, *which* sets they are;[25] and so on. (This is an instance of the phenomenon I called "conceptual relativity" in the last lecture.) So much about the identity relations between different *categories* of mathematical objects is conventional, that the picture of ourselves as describing a bunch of objects that are there "anyway" is in trouble from the start.

Second, talk of *existence* in mathematics is fungible with talk of possibility—not "possibility" in some metaphysical sense, but *mathematical* possibility, possibility in a sense that we understand from mathematics itself. Every statement about the "existence" of any mathematical entities is equivalent (equivalent mathematically, and equivalent from the point of view of application as well) with a statement that doesn't assert the actual existence of any mathematical objects at all, but only asserts the *mathematical possibility* of certain structures.[26]

Mathematical truth strongly resembles logical truth, as Frege already argued, and, indeed, Frege's philosophy was brilliantly summarized many years ago by Georg Kreisel,[27] when he said that the question is not the existence of mathematical objects but the objectivity of mathematics. Everything about the success of mathematics, and the deep dependence of much contemporary science, including physics, but not only physics, *on* mathematics, supports taking mathematical theorems as objective truths; but nothing supports taking mathematical theorems as descriptions of a special realm of "abstract entities," and nothing is gained, in philosophy of mathematics or elsewhere, by so doing.

Methodological Value Judgments

I want finally to say a word about a class of value judgments that is often overlooked, value judgments that are internal to scientific inquiry itself: judgments of *coherence, simplicity, plausibility,* and the like. An example for the indispensability of such judgments is the following: both Einstein's General Relativity and Alfred North Whitehead's theory of gravita-

tion (of which most people have never heard!) agreed
with Special Relativity, and both predicted the familiar phenomena of the deflection of light by gravitation, the non-
Newtonian character of the orbit of Mercury, the exact orbit
of the Moon, and so on. Yet Einstein's theory was accepted
and Whitehead's theory was rejected fifty years before anyone thought of an observation that would decide between
the two.[28] The judgment that scientists explicitly or implicitly made, that Whitehead's theory was too "implausible"
or too "ad hoc" to be taken seriously, was clearly a *value
judgment.* The similarity of judgments of this kind to aesthetic judgments has often been pointed out, and, indeed,
Dirac was famous for saying that certain theories should be
taken seriously because they were "beautiful," while others
couldn't possibly be true because they were "ugly." If we
were to imitate G. E. Moore's *Principia Ethica,* we would
have to say that there are "simple non-natural qualities" of
beauty, and ugliness, and that what the scientist does, in de-
ciding which theories (among those not ruled out by the
evidence) are worth testing, is to perceive, by means of some
sort of non-natural "intuition," which theories possess the
one non-natural quality and which possess the other, a move
which would be a form of "Platonism."

Once again, I suggest that such "Platonism" is uncalled
for. We needn't think that we are describing non-natural
properties when we say that a theory is beautiful or simple
or coherent. What we are doing is extremely complex, but
here is a rough account: just as the ethically important ad-
jectives "cruel" and "compassionate" describe properties
that human beings may have or lack, not supernatural properties, but also not properties that one can simply perceive

(or "measure") without having understood and learned to imaginatively identify with a particular evaluative outlook, so "simple" and "coherent" (in their scientific applications) describe properties that certain human products, scientific theories, may have or lack, and that one cannot perceive without having understood and learned to imaginatively identify with a particular evaluative outlook. And just as the primary point of the judgment that someone is cruel is usually to evaluate rather than merely to describe (although, on some occasions, it *can* be used merely to describe), so the primary point of the judgment that a theory or an explanation is simple or coherent is usually to evaluate rather than merely to describe (although on some occasions it can be used merely to describe). This kind of evaluation is fallible and often controversial, but it is a kind that good scientists learn to make. Indeed, becoming a successful scientist, especially a successful theoretician, is largely a matter of developing a capacity to make such judgments through a process of learning, both formal learning but even more learning in the course of one's scientific experience, just as learning to compose outstanding pieces of music is a matter of developing a perhaps partly inborn capacity through formal learning but even more learning in the course of one's musical experience.

Moreover, there is something not unrelated to *logic* here; for the judgment as to which theories are *plausible enough* (given considerations of "simplicity," "coherence with background knowledge," "beauty," and the like) to even merit testing, and which theories are not, is essential to the various sorts of non-deductive inference that we encounter in the natural sciences and in everyday problem-solving. Of course, this immense class of non-deductive inferences has never been formalized in the way that deductive inference has, and I myself see no reason to think that it could be. But deduction and non-deductive inference, of whatever sort, have this in common: they are exercises in *reasoning*. And what leads to "Platonizing" is yielding to the temptation to find mysterious entities which somehow guarantee or stand behind correct judgments of the reasonable and the unreasonable.

In my next and final lecture in this series I will discuss ethical judgments, and then will come back to the supposed philosophical subject of Ontology—which I have been discussing implicitly all along as well, by arguing that it doesn't *do* anything for us in ethics or philosophy of mathematics or philosophy of logic or theory of scientific method—and pronounce an "obituary" upon it.

"Ontology": An Obituary

In the previous lecture I said that logical statements and methodological value judgments could be described as "judgments of the reasonable and the unreasonable." But most ethical judgments are also judgments of the reasonable and the unreasonable—not in the Platonic sense, the sense of what is required by Reason conceived of as a transcendent metaphysical faculty, but in the sense of what is and what is not reasonable given the concerns of the ethical life, as I described them in my first lecture. Of course, it sometimes happens that when people disagree—for example, on the extent to which a given society should be a "welfare state"— one side in the dispute is simply using ethical language as a rhetorical cover for self-interest; but it would be arrogant and unfair to suppose that this is always the case. It can also be the case that both parties in the dispute are genuinely kind, sympathetic, and concerned for the common welfare (not as something dogmatically defined in advance, but as something open to discussion and argument), and that what

they disagree upon is how it is *reasonable* for people with
these very concerns to act in a particular concrete situation.

I have two purposes in comparing such ethical judgments
to methodological value judgments: to point out, first, that
those forms of extreme "naturalism" that deny all objectivity
to ethical valuings should, in consistency, deny all objectivity
to methodological valuings as well—a position that (*pace*
Richard Rorty!)[1] no one should embrace.[2] My second purpose is to suggest that the point that "the question is the objectivity of the discourse in question, and not the existence
of some realm of non-natural objects"[3] applies to valuings in
general, and not only to philosophy of logic and mathematics. If ethical statements are, as I urge, forms of reflection
that are as fully governed by norms of truth and validity as
any other form of cognitive activity, the reason is that
reflection on how it is reasonable to act given the overall
concerns of the ethical life—even with all the tensions between those concerns that I mentioned in my first lecture—
is subject to the same standards of fallibilistic inquiry that all
practical reasoning is subject to,[4] and the notions of truth
and validity are internal to practical reasoning itself.

Ethical Judgments

So now we have come (as I promised we would) to the case
of ethical statements.

The first thing I want to say is that if Wittgenstein was
right in saying that "mathematics is a motley," then ethics is,
so to speak, a motley *squared.* This may explain why philosophers who write about the subject so often ignore vast tracts
of ethical judgment. There are many different *kinds* of ethi-

cal judgments. For example, there are ethical judgments which involve praise or blame and ethical judgments which have nothing to do with praise and blame[5] (an example of the latter, which is of historical importance, is the judgment that the Lisbon earthquake of 1755 was a very bad thing; this is also a counterexample to the idea that all ethical judgments have the function of "prescribing" conduct); there are ethical judgments which imply "oughts" and ethical judgments which do not imply "oughts"; and there are a host of ethical judgments which are not happily formulated using the moral philosopher's favorite words, *ought, must, mustn't, good, bad, right, wrong, duty,* and *obligation*—the idea that all ethical issues can be expressed in this meager vocabulary is a form of philosophical blindness.[6] In addition, the concerns of ethics range from the statement of very abstract principles, such as principles of human rights, to the solution of situated and highly specific practical problems.[7]

I have said that logical truths are not descriptions. One cannot say equally simply that ethical truths are not descriptions, because it is a matter of *which* ethical statements one has in mind. The statement that "Vlad the Impaler was an exceptionally cruel monarch," or the statement that "The cruelties of the regime provoked a number of rebellions," statements one can imagine encountering in a work of history, *are* descriptions; they are descriptions of, respectively, Vlad the Impaler and the causes of certain historical events, certain rebellions. (They are not, of course, descriptions of Plato's "Forms.") But "Terrorism is criminal" and "Wife-beating is wrong" aren't descriptions; they are simply evaluations that convey moral condemnation. (The historian's statements may also do this, to a certain extent, but I doubt that the *purpose* of the historian would be to perform the speech-act of "condemning" these long-dead persons; rather, his aim is to make the historical events intelligible, and to do this he employs a *description which is itself made available by a moral point of view.*)[8] Indeed, I don't think "The Lisbon earthquake was a terrible event" is likely to have been a *description*—although it might be if offered in response to the question, "Was the Lisbon earthquake a bad one?"—but as normally used by people who already know the magnitude of the Lisbon earthquake, this sentence is yet another sort of moral evaluation, one which assesses the moral significance of an event without assigning praise or blame.

In short (and here I will find it convenient to use the term *valuings* as a general term for value judgments of every sort), my position isn't simply that "valuings are not descriptions"; my position is that *some* valuings, in fact, some ethical valuings, *are* descriptions (though not of anything "non-natural"), and *some* valuings are not descriptions. Valuings do not contrast *simply* with descriptions; there is an overlap, in my view, between the class of descriptions and the class of valuings.

There is, however, a further issue to be discused, one that is inescapable in any discussion of the issue about whether we should or shouldn't seek a metaphysical foundation for ethics, and that is the fact that ethical claims are so frequently *controversial*. If ethical claims are objective—or, better, to use the language Conant employed in describing my position, if they are *bona fide* instances of assertoric discourse, forms of reflection that are as fully governed by norms of truth and validity as any other form of cognitive activity—how is it that we so often can't agree on which ones are true?

The Question of Ethical Disagreement

There is a way in which the cards are regularly "stacked" when this question is asked; it is assumed, that is, that questions of fact are, by their very nature, such that we can come to agreement about them (and perhaps such that we even *tend to* come into agreement about them). This idea was, famously, made the centerpiece of C. S. Peirce's version of pragmatism. This idea is, I think, quite unwarranted, as is the idea that all ethical questions are, by their very nature, controversial.

First of all, there are ethical issues about which people who stand within the ethical life at all do agree. That killing of the innocent, cheating, robbery, etc., are wrong is something accepted by morally conscious people everywhere. But the disagreement comes about for a reason I pointed out in my first lecture: that real ethical questions are a species of practical question, and practical questions don't only involve valuings, they involve a complex mixture of philosophical beliefs, religious beliefs, and factual beliefs as well. Consider, for example, the controversy about abortion—a controversy which is often cited as an example of purely ethical disagreement (and, moreover, "in principle irresolvable" ethical disagreement).[9] Disagreements about the morality of abortion are usually also disagreements about the question of just when a fetus becomes a person—sometimes this is put in metaphysical terms, as "When does the fetus acquire a soul?" To assume that the irresolvability—if it *is* irresolvable—of

the question of the legitimacy of abortion is simply an example of the "irresolvability" of ethical disputes, and not, for
example, an example of the irresolvability of *metaphysical*
disputes, is, on the face of it, unwarranted.

We needn't consider cases of religious disagreement to
make the same point; many practical questions involve factual estimates on which it is difficult if not impossible to
ever get convergence. Whether, for example, a fully socialist
society—that is, one which did not allow large private busi-
nesses and corporations—*could* exist and be peaceful, economically successful, and democratic, is, by anybody's lights,
an *empirical* question, but it is an empirical question on
which we are unlikely to ever get agreement, unless, that is,
such a society actually comes into existence at some time,
and *is* peaceful, economically successful, and democratic.
(We all know that there have been fully socialist societies
which were neither economically successful nor democratic,
but that hardly settles the possibility-question to the satisfaction of all social thinkers.) If the power of pro-capitalist
forces is sufficiently great to prevent such a society from ever
being tried again in the future, or if socialist experiments are
tried only in impoverished and backward countries, and fail
there, it is unlikely that there will ever be agreement on
"what would have happened if." And even in cases where the
relevant experiment is tried—not, of course, the experiment
of a fully socialist society, but some other social experiment—and the experiment is successful, questions as to
whether the same thing would work the next time, or in the
next case, are frequently highly controversial, and the model
of everyone ultimately converging to one view has, as far as I
can see, no relation to reality. What we can tell at best, if we

try something in connection with a social problem and it works well—for example, if a national health plan, of the kind that exists in many European countries, continues to work well in most of those countries—it is unlikely to be conceded by those who oppose such a plan that it would work well in the United States. And, while I myself am strongly in favor of having such a plan in the United States, I do recognize that there are cases in which something works well in one country and the "same" thing does not work well in another country. In short, my view is that the impossibility of getting clean-cut "verifications" that something is the right thing to do, even when the success-criteria are agreed upon—unless, that is, you have actually *done* it, and it has "worked" to everyone's satisfaction—is a general feature of practical problem resolution. If we see ethical decision as a special case of practical decision, as I argued in my first lecture, then we should not be surprised or dismayed by the extent to which controversy arises in connection with it.

As is obvious, I have not, in these last remarks or in Part I as a whole, attempted to discuss all the issues that I have discussed in other places, in particular, the issues that I discuss in *The Collapse of the Fact/Value Dichotomy*. What I have been concerned to do just now and in the previous lecture is to speak about one *metaphysical* reason that has led many philosophers to deny the objectivity of ethical judgment, namely that it doesn't *fit the picture* of "description of natural facts." I have argued that, indeed, it is *right* that certain crucial ethical statements are not descriptions, but that that is no reason for classifying them as outside the range of the notions of truth and falsity, good and bad argument, and the like. To recognize that there can be "objectivity without objects," and that a *bona fide* statement is not necessarily a *description*, is essential to clear thinking about these issues.

The Revival of Ontology by Quine

So far I have argued that the denial of the possibility of objective judgment in any of the cases in which we have objectivity without objects has disastrous consequences. For example, the metaphysical *reasons* which are offered for denying the very possibility of objective ethical judgment (as I have argued in a number of places, and briefly argued in this volume as well) would equally imply the impossibility of objective methodological value judgments, and thereby threaten the objectivity of science itself; on the other hand, in each of these cases, to account for the objectivity of the discourse in question by positing non-natural objects (even if they are called "abstract entities") is to offer a pseudo-explanation. In addition, attempts at explaining the objectivity of the various discourses I have discussed by *reducing* those discourses to other (supposedly "unproblematic") discourses are also well known to have failed.

If, then, Ontology in all three of the forms I distinguished in my opening lecture—inflationary, reductionist, and eliminationist—has been a failure, "How come," the reader may wonder, "it is precisely in *analytic* philosophy—a kind of philosophy that, for many years, was *hostile* to the very word 'ontology'—that Ontology flourishes?"

If we ask *when* Ontology became a respectable subject for an analytic philosopher to pursue, the mystery disappears. It became respectable in 1948, when Quine published a famous paper titled "On What There Is."[10] It was Quine who single-handedly made Ontology a respectable subject. (In the Continental tradition, of course, the *word* "ontology" was employed by Heidegger, but, as I discussed briefly in the first lecture, not in the very traditional sense—which Heidegger scorned as "ontotheology"—in which Quine consciously used it.)[11]

Although there are many difficult issues about the exact interpretation of that great essay (as there are about the major writings of any great philosopher), I can tell you just how bowled over I was when I read it as a first-year graduate student in 1948–49; and I think my reaction was not untypical. What was impressive, in my eyes, *wasn't* the technical criterion of "ontological commitment" in that paper, a criterion to which so many pages of commentary by so many philosophers have been devoted. What was impressive were one or two very simple-seeming arguments. First, Quine called our attention to the fact that we use the word "exist" in mathematics—or, if you want to quibble about whether this is really a characteristic or essential feature of mathematics, Quine said, virtually in these words,[12] "All right, I'll *give you* the word 'exist,' and just stick to 'there are.'" Who could deny that we say things like "There are prime numbers greater than a million"? and "For every *n* there are prime numbers greater than *n*"? (Saying such things is called "quantifying over numbers" by Quine.)

(That we don't say, "There are numbers" *simpliciter* in mathematics did not seem important to me then, of course.)

Second, Quine pointed to two ways one might try to minimize the significance of the fact—of which he had just convinced me—that in mathematics one speaks as if numbers exist (speaks as if there are numbers). One way of minimiz-

ing the significance of the fact that we "quantify over numbers" is to say that speaking this way is "just a manner of
speaking" *without* showing any way of *explaining* the supposed "mere *façon de parler*" in any other terms. Put like
that, it sounds like a form of philosophical cheating, mere
"hand-waving." (The Heideggerian strategy of simply denying that science has any serious significance for our understanding of "Being" is another form of such hand-waving.)

The other way is to provide a genuine *replacement,* a *substitute for,* the *façon de parler* in some other idiom. And this
can be done: for the numbers it is possible to substitute certain sets of sets of . . . —for short, certain set-theoretic constructions—to the satisfaction of mathematicians. For
mathematical purposes, *all* mathematical entities can be
"identified with" (i.e., *replaced by*) certain sets. So someone
who is willing to "posit" (a term Quine used in key places in
"On What There Is") sets, but refuses to posit numbers in
addition to sets, does not have to "cheat" or "wave his
hands"—he can say, "*This* is exactly how I will replace my
talk of 'numbers' if you challenge me; but for everyday purposes, such as counting my change, I will go on talking of
'numbers.'" In effect, Quine said: "If you are going to claim
that talk of so-and-sos (I have used numbers as my example,
but the point is quite general) is a mere 'manner of speaking,' then show me how to *replace* the manner of speaking. If
you can't, you are cheating."

Well, it *is* possible to replace talk of numbers with talk of
sets. But what about sets? Here Quine is a reluctant Platonist
("I have felt that if I must come to terms with Platonism, the
least I can do is keep it extensional").[13] He is a Platonist because physics needs mathematics, and so, if he is going to as-

sert the propositions of our best contemporary science, he will find himself quantifying over sets. And to say "I quantify over them, but I am not saying they *really* exist" would be just another form of the hand-waving that it was the point of "On What There Is" to forswear.

As a 22-year-old graduate student—and for a long time thereafter—I was utterly convinced! To be a good philosopher (and part of being a good philosopher is, of course, to take science seriously) I must face up to the need to accept "the existence of abstract entities."

Problems in the Desert Landscape

But a number of problems were hidden just below the surface of the simple-seeming argument I have rehearsed here. We have just seen that ontology was made respectable, in analytic philosophy, by Quine's idea that you could read it off of the existential commitments of your theory, which he thought was the unified scientific theory of everything. But we have also seen that if you leave Quine's scientism to one side, you will realize that we don't have a single, unified theory of the world off of which to read our ontology. It is true, for example, that numbers can be "identified with" sets. But, as I pointed out in the second lecture, they can also be identified with *functions* (as they were, for example, by Alonzo Church in his "calculi of lambda-conversion"). These different ways of *formalizing* mathematics do not have any metaphysical significance at all, to the working mathematician at least. What attitude should we take to these "equivalent optional languages," as I called them? This question is one concerning which Quine subsequently vacillated, by his own admission.[14] I have argued in this volume that to suppose that there is a serious question of "the real existence of sets" is silly.

Moreover, at a certain point I pointed out (and my suggestion was worked out in a much more extensive way first by Charles Parsons and more recently by Geoffrey Hellman) that we can avoid quantifying over abstract entities in mathematics entirely, by formalizing mathematics in a *modal logical language,* one which takes as primitive (mathematical) *possibility* and *necessity.* Quine, in writings late in his life, became aware of this, and rejected it for an interesting reason—rejected it, not as an impossible formalization of mathematics, but as one that *makes ontological commitments unclear.*[15] In other words, unless you formalize mathematics in precisely the kind of logic to which his criterion of ontological commitment applies, then you are somehow cheating! The very idea that the modalities have (or may have) *hidden* "ontological commitments" shows just how deep the Platonist bug had bitten Quine by this time.

But I want now to focus on a different, and much more generally intelligible issue—as I fear this talk of the "ontological commitments of mathematics" may not be. What of the "ontological commitments" of *non*-scientific language?

Ontology and Non-Scientific Language

We say such things as this: "Some passages in Kant's writing are difficult to interpret." No one has proposed a *replacement* for such talk (in the sense in which identifying numbers with certain sets is suggesting a replacement for quantification over "unreduced" numbers). No doubt, Quine himself would agree that some passages in Kant's writing are difficult to interpret. So shouldn't Quine, by just the reasoning of "On What There Is," agree that he is committed to the *existence* of such things as "passages which are difficult to interpret," and, more generally, of such things as correct and incorrect interpretations of passages? But, at least from the publication of *Word and Object* (1960), Quine introduced another move—one suspiciously like the move he repudiated in "On What There Is." The move is to say that certain entities we quantify over, and certain predicates we use, are indeed indispensable in everyday language, but these quantifications, and the use of these predicates, *have no ontological significance.* In fine, Quine distinguished between a first-class conceptual system (science, or rather science properly formalized) and what he called "a second-grade system,"[16] and he simply ruled that only our first-grade conceptual system represents an account of what the world contains that we can and must take seriously (in a fallibilistic spirit, of course). Since nothing in the conceptual scheme of physics, for example, corresponds to a *meaning fact,* the closest we can come to such facts, according to Quine, is bare behaviorist psychology in the style of Skinner. And if Skinnerian psychology cannot provide an account of meaning or reference, so much the worse for meaning and reference! Stated so baldly, this is, of course, more a caricature of Quine's views than an exposition of them; but I believe that it captures what is essentially wrong. I think it is fair to say that from *Word and Object* on, the argumentation of "On What There Is" ceases to do very much work for Quine, and what does the real work is a premise he shares with such philosophers as Bernard Williams[17] and Simon Blackburn[18] and

Paul Churchland, the premise that it is only our best *scientific* theory of the world that says anything we can take seriously about what there is.

But what is wrong with saying that it is only our best scientific theory of the world that says anything about what there is? The philosophers I just mentioned do not consider the interpretation of texts to be a matter of a scientific theory (as indeed it isn't). So the statement about Kant isn't part of our best scientific theory of the world—it isn't part of *any* "theory." Are you really prepared to conclude with Paul Churchland that *passages which are difficult to interpret do not exist*? That believing that there are passages which are difficult to interpret is like believing an outmoded scientific theory, like believing in phlogiston, caloric, and the four principles of medieval alchemy?[19] Isn't there something *mad* about such a conclusion? Or should we conclude with Bernard Williams that such beliefs are only true "relative to some social world or other," whatever *that* means? Or should we be "quasi-realists" about them with Simon Blackburn? How high the seas of language run!

Ontology: The Obituary

I know I will not convince true believers, but if I can inoculate some readers against this particular disease I shall be more than happy. What we see in this brief account of the revival of Ontology within the supposedly chaste precincts of analytic philosophy is something that I have been trying to point out from my second lecture in this series: that once we assume that there is, somehow fixed in advance, a single "real," a single "literal" sense of "exist"—and, by the way, a single "literal" sense of "identity"—one which is cast in marble, and cannot be either contracted or expanded without defiling the statue of the god, we are already wandering in Cloud Cuckoo Land. That assumption is implicit in Quine's procedure from the start—hence the hostility to modal logic, even when the modalities are as clear as the *mathematical* senses of "possible" and "impossible," which seems to Quine just a way of somehow *concealing* what we are saying "exists" in this literal sense; hence the wholesale dismissal of our "second grade [conceptual] system," which he sees not as illustrating the endless possibilities of extending our notions of "existence" (Conceptual Pluralism) but rather as just so much loose talk. I promised an obituary on Ontology, but to extend these remarks would not be so much an obituary as flogging a dead horse. Instead, I shall just say this (since it *is* customary to say at least one good word about the dead): even if Ontology has become a stinking corpse, in Plato and Aristotle it represented the vehicle for conveying many genuine philosophical insights. The insights still preoccupy all of us in philosophy who have any historical sense at all. But the vehicle has long since outlived its usefulness.

PART II

Enlightenment and Pragmatism

The Three Enlightenments

A well-known dialogue of Plato's begins with an encounter between Socrates and Euthyphro, who, it turns out, is on his way to a trial.[1] Socrates naturally asks, "Your case, Euthyphro? What is it? Are you prosecuting or defending?" "Prosecuting," Euthyphro replies.

> Socrates: Whom?
>
> Euthyphro: One whom I am thought a maniac to be attacking.
>
> Socrates: How so. Is it someone who has wings to fly away with?
>
> Euthyphro: He is far from being able to do that; he happens to be a very old man.
>
> Socrates: Who is it, then?
>
> Euthyphro: It is my father.
>
> Socrates: Your father, my good friend?
>
> Euthyphro: Just so.
>
> Socrates: What is the complaint? Of what do you accuse him?

Euthyphro: Of murder, Socrates.

Socrates: Good heavens, Euthyphro! Surely the crowd is ignorant of the way things ought to go. I fancy it is not correct for any ordinary person to do that [to prosecute his father on this charge]; but only for a man far advanced in point of wisdom.

Euthyphro: Yes, Socrates, by heaven! Far advanced!

After this self-congratulatory reply, Euthyphro proceeds to tell Socrates that "the victim in this case was a laborer of mine, and when we were cultivating land in Naxos, we employed him on our farm. One day he had been drinking, and became enraged at one of our domestics and cut his throat, whereupon my father bound him hand and foot and threw him into a ditch. Then he sent a man to Athens to find out from the seer what ought to be done—meanwhile paying no attention to the man who had been bound, neglecting him because he was a murderer and it would be no great matter even if he died. And that is what happened."

And so Euthyphro has taken it upon himself to charge his own father for murder. Moreover, Euthyphro is absolutely certain that this is demanded by "piety."

Socrates soon opens the philosophical action of the dialogue by saying, "But you, by heaven! Euthyphro, you think that you have such an accurate knowledge of things divine, and what is pious and what is impious, that, in circumstances such as you describe, you can accuse your father? You are not afraid that you yourself are doing an impious deed?" The response is: "Why Socrates, if I did not have an accurate knowledge of all that, I should be good for nothing, and Euthyphro would be no different from the general run of men."

In the course of the discussion, Socrates very soon asks Euthyphro, "How do you define the pious and the impious?"—and Euthyphro replies: "Well then, I say that pious is what I am now doing, prosecuting the wrongdoer who commits a murder or a sacrilegious robbery, or sins in any point like that, whether it be your father, your mother, or whoever it may be. And not to prosecute would be impious." And then he proceeds to give Socrates what he calls a "decisive proof" of the truth of his words, namely that Zeus is regarded by man as the best and most just of the gods, and yet Zeus bound his father, Cronos, because he wickedly devoured his (other) sons.

To this Socrates replies, "There, Euthyphro, you have the reason why the charge [of impiety] is brought against me. It is because, whenever people tell such stories about the gods, I am prone to take it ill, and so they will maintain that I am sinful. Well now, if you who are so well versed in matters of the sort entertain the same beliefs, then necessarily, it would seem, I must give in, for what could we urge who admit that, for our own part, we are quite ignorant about these matters? But, in the name of friendship, tell me! Do you actually believe that these things happened so?"

This short dialogue of Plato's (including the famous question which is at its heart, whether actions are pious because the gods approve of them, or whether the gods approve of them because they are pious) is a beautiful representative in miniature of the very beginning of the Western tradition of philosophy as we know it. Those of you who have read it will know that Socrates does not pretend to have an *answer* to the difficult question of the nature of piety. Rather, what he claims is that it is not a sufficient answer to the question to give a list of actions that are conventionally regarded as pious and a list of those that are conventionally regarded as impious—and certainly not a sufficient answer to appeal to the Greek analogue of revelation, the stories about the gods.

Philosophy, in this dialogue, already represents what I shall call reflective transcendence, that is, standing back from conventional opinion, on the one hand, and the authority of revelation (i.e., of literally and uncritically accepted religious texts or myths) on the other, and asking "Why?" Philosophy, as we already see it here, thus combines two aspirations: the aspiration to justice, and the aspiration to critical thinking. Of course, Euthyphro, in his own way, seeks justice; indeed, he is convinced that no one knows better than himself what the demands of justice are. What Euthyphro fails to appreciate is the need to connect the aspiration to justice with the practice of critical and independent thinking, without which the search for justice can so easily become—as indeed it does in Euthyphro's case—a cover for fanaticism.

If you will now permit me to jump about two millennia, to the seventeenth and eighteenth centuries of the common era, and particularly to the phenomenon that historians have called the "Enlightenment," we can see one development of the idea of linking the search for justice and the practice of reflective transcendence, of "standing back." Broadly speaking, the Enlightenment was characterized by two great forces.

One force, the influence of the new philosophies of Hobbes and Locke in England, and of Rousseau, as well as of Continental Rationalism, manifested itself in the new conception of society as a "social contract," and in the new talk of "natural rights." Both continue to be important in today's discussions in political theory.[2] But apart from the details, and apart even from the question as to how social contract theory is to be understood, we can say that the lasting effect of the social contract conception—one that we tend to take for granted—is the widespread acceptance of the idea that governments derive their legitimacy from the consent of the governed; while the lasting effect of the Enlightenment's talk of natural rights is the prevalence of the idea that every human being should have the opportunity to develop certain capabilities (particularly those capabilities needed to play the role of an autonomous citizen in a democratic polity).[3]

The second great force that characterized the Enlightenment was the new science. The enormous successes of Newtonian physics impressed a wide public, even if that public was incapable then (as most of us are now) of following the mathematical and other technicalities of the new science. As Crane Brinton put it: "No doubt the ladies and gentlemen who admired Newton were for the most part incapable of understanding the *Principia;* and, if some of them fashionably dabbled at home with scientific experiments, they had no very sophisticated concepts of scientific method. Science was for them, however, living, growing evidence that human beings, using their 'natural' reasoning powers in a fairly obvious and teachable way, could not only understand the way things really are in the universe; they could understand what human beings are really like, and by combining this knowledge of nature and human nature, learn to live happier and better lives."[4]

However vague all of these ideas may be (and certainly

they admit of a large number of very different interpretations), as Brinton also remarks, "Certainly very specific, and often very successful, reform movements sprang directly from the thinkers of the Enlightenment. Beccaria's *On Crimes and Punishments* helped set Bentham's mind to work on problems of law reform, and the two together, along with many others, inspired humane reforms in criminal law and in prisons, as well as efficient reforms in civil law all over the western world."[5]

If we compare the seventeenth- and eighteenth-century enlightenment, the Enlightenment with a capital "E," with the earlier Platonic enlightenment, it is not hard to perceive both similarities and differences. On the side of the similarities, there is the same aspiration to reflective transcendence, the same willingness to criticize conventional beliefs and institutions, and to propose radical reforms.

When I speak of a willingness to propose radical reforms in connection with Plato, I don't mean only the grand scheme of the *Republic* as a whole, but more specifically Plato's criticism of the idea of the innate inferiority of women.[6] You may recall that Socrates considers the objection that "the natures of men and women are different, and yet we are now saying that these different natures are to have the same occupations." The part of the discussion I want to quote begins with Socrates' remark about the effect on people of the practice of debating:

> It is extraordinary, Glaucon, what an effect the practice of debating has upon people.
> Why do you say that?
> Because they often seem to fall unconsciously into mere disputes about words which they mistake for reasonable argument, through being unable to draw the distinctions

proper to the subject; and so instead of a philosophical exchange of ideas, they go off in chase of contradictions which are purely verbal.

Socrates explains the point thus:[7]

> We have been strenuously insisting on the letter of our principle that different natures should not have the same occupations, as if we were scoring a point in a debate; but we have altogether neglected to consider what sort of sameness or difference we meant and in what respect these natures and occupations were to be defined as different or the same. Consequently, we might very well be asking one another whether there is not an opposition between bald and long-haired men, and, when that was admitted, forbid one set to be shoemakers, if the other were following that trade.
>
> That would be absurd.
>
> Yes, but only because we never meant any and every sort of sameness or difference in nature, but the sort that was relevant to the occupations in question. We meant, for instance, that a man and a woman have the same nature if both have a talent for medicine; whereas two men have different natures if one is a born physician, the other a born carpenter.
>
> Yes, of course.
>
> If, then, we find that either the male sex or the female is specially qualified for any particular form of occupation, then that occupation, we shall say, ought to be assigned to one sex or the other. But if the only difference appears to be that the male begets and the woman brings forth, we shall conclude that no difference between man and woman has yet been produced that is relevant to our purpose. We shall continue to think it proper for our Guardians and their wives to share in the same pursuits.[8]

The similarities between the Platonic enlightenment and the seventeenth- and eighteenth-century Enlightenment extend farther: there is the same enthusiasm for the new science (in Plato's case, enthusiasm for Euclidean geometry), and there is the same refusal to allow questions of ethics and political philosophy to be decided by an appeal to religious texts and/or myths. Yet there is also a very large difference.

In Plato's view, what makes a state (ideally) legitimate is that it is ruled by a class of people (who must be philosophers) who alone have the capacity to discern reliably the nature of the Good—which, in Greek thought, means above all the nature of the best life for human beings—*together with* the requirement that the other components of the state function properly under the guidance of the philosopher-rulers. Legitimacy (or, in Plato's terms, "justice") depends upon the presence of a properly functioning meritocracy, not on the consent of the governed.[9]

I want now to talk about a *third* "enlightenment"—one that hasn't happened yet, or hasn't at any rate fully happened, but one that I hope *will* happen, and one worth struggling for. More than any other thinker of the last century, I think that John Dewey is the best philosopher of this enlightenment (I shall call it the *pragmatist* enlightenment).

Like the two previous enlightenments, the pragmatist enlightenment valorizes reflective transcendence, or, to use an expression Dewey himself once used, *criticism of criticisms.*[10] (By "criticism of criticisms," which, in his *Human Nature and Conduct,* Dewey equated with philosophy, he meant not just the criticism of received ideas, but higher-level criticism, the "standing back" and criticizing even the ways in which we are accustomed to criticize ideas, the criticism of our ways of criticism.) Like the two previous enlightenments, the pragmatist enlightenment is willing to be nonconform-

ist, and willing to advocate radical reform. Like the eighteenth-century enlightenment, it rejects Plato's meritocratic
model for an ideal society; indeed, the case against that
model has rarely been better stated than by Dewey in the following words:

> History shows that there have been benevolent despots who
> wish to bestow blessings upon others. They have not suc-
> ceeded, except when their efforts have taken the indirect
> form of changing the conditions under which those live who
> are disadvantageously placed. The same principle holds of re-
> formers and philanthropists when they try to do good to oth-
> ers in ways which leave passive those to be benefited. There is
> a moral tragedy inherent in efforts to further the common
> good which prevent the result from being either good or
> common—not good, because it is at the expense of the active
> growth of those to be helped, and not common because these
> have no share in bringing the result about.[11]

However, the pragmatist enlightenment is not a mere
continuation of the seventeenth- and eighteenth-century
Enlightenment, although it certainly builds on the democratic strain in the Enlightenment. What Dewey calls for has
been described by Robert Westbrook as "deliberative democracy,"[12] and the term is apt. But Dewey's vision of how
deliberative democracy could work is not an eighteenth-
century one. The difference will be easier to explain if I first
say something about the other feature of enlightenment, the
valorization of reason, which was present in different forms
in Plato and in the Enlightenment (with a capital "E").

Dewey does not, in fact, like the term "reason" very much
(certainly not the term "Reason" with a capital "R"), prefer-
ring to speak of the application of *intelligence* to problems,

and the change in terminology is symptomatic of a deep criticism of traditional philosophy. "Reason," in the traditional sense, was, above all, a faculty by means of which human beings were supposed to be able to arrive at one or another set of immutable truths. It is true that this conception had already been criticized by the empiricists, but the empiricist criticism of reason seemed seriously flawed to Dewey. Dewey, surprisingly—at first, at least to people with a conventional philosophical education—finds traditional empiricism in its own way as aprioristic as traditional rationalism.

Traditional rationalism, famously, thinks the general form of scientific explanations can be known a priori: we know a priori the laws of geometry and even the fundamental principles of mechanics, according to Descartes. But empiricism equally thinks that the general form of scientific data, indeed of all empirical data, can be known a priori—even if it doesn't say so in so many words! From Locke, Berkeley, and Hume down to Ernst Mach, empiricists held that all empirical data consists of "sensations," conceived of as an unconceptualized given against which putative knowledge claims can be checked. Against this view William James had already insisted that while all perceptual experience has both conceptual and non-conceptual aspects, the attempt to divide any experience which is a recognition of something into parts is futile: "Sensations and apperceptive idea fuse here so intimately [in a 'presented and recognized material object'] that you can no more tell where one begins and the other ends, than you can tell, in those cunning circular panoramas that have lately been exhibited, where the real foreground and the painted canvas join together."[13] Dewey, continuing the line of thought that James had begun, insists that by creating new observation-concepts we "institute" new data. Modern physics (and of course not only physics) has richly born him out. A scientist may speak of observing a proton colliding with a nucleus, or of observing a virus with the aid of an electron microscope, or of observing genes or black holes, and so forth. *Neither the form of possible explanations nor the form of possible data can be fixed in advance, once and for all.*

Pragmatism in general (and not only Deweyan pragmatism) is characterized by being simultaneously *fallibilist* and *anti-skeptical,* whereas traditional empiricism is seen by pragmatists as oscillating between being too skeptical, in one moment, and insufficiently fallibilist in another of its moments.

Dewey often calls for more investigation—empirical, policy-oriented investigation—of social problems, but it is important to realize that the social-scientific research Dewey longed for was social science in the service of ordinary people, who, after all, know best when and where their shoe pinches.

Among the classic empiricist thinkers, the most famous ones to call before John Dewey did for the application of scientific research to the problems of society were Mill and Comte. But Comte reverted to meritocracy. He visualized handing social problems over to *savants,* social-scientific intellectuals, a move which falls under Dewey's criticism of the idea of the "benevolent despot."

It might seem that this same criticism cannot be voiced against Mill, who, as much as Dewey was to do, valued active participation in all aspects of the democratic process. But as far as the application of social-scientific knowledge to social problems is concerned, what Mill called for was the development of a perfected science of *individual psychology*, from which, he thought—continuing the tradition of methodological individualism so characteristic of classical empiricism—we would be able to derive social laws (via the hoped-for reduction of sociology to psychology) which could then be applied to particular social problems. This entire program, as most would concede today, is a misguided fantasy.

On Dewey's view, then, the philosophers of the Enlightenment fell into one of two errors: either they attempted to reason aprioristically, which is to say dogmatically, at one or another crucial point; or (especially if they were empiricists) they fabulated an imaginary science of sensationalistical psychology instead of trying to develop real scientific knowledge of real social processes.[14] Dewey has often been accused of being "scientistic"; not only is the criticism unjust (as anyone who has read his *Art as Experience* or *Human Nature and Conduct* knows), but it fails to see that Dewey is reacting against a long tradition of social thought which is utterly lacking in respect for serious empirical study of social problems. Even Karl Marx, who claimed to have discovered the "laws" of capitalist development, did not resist the temptation to give an a priori proof in volume 3 of his *Capital* that capitalism *must* collapse of its alleged internal contradictions![15]

I now turn to a second—and equally important—point of difference between the seventeenth- and eighteenth-century Enlightenment and the pragmatist enlightenment. In the article I quoted from earlier, Brinton very early on tells us that "two major themes in the history of philosophy took on special importance as they were absorbed into the thinking of the educated public of the Enlightenment."[16] The second "theme," which I chose to discuss first, was "the increasing prestige of natural science," and the remarkable way in which that prestige was reflected in an increasing faith in the power of reason to solve human problems. The first theme was, in Brinton's description, that "the development [in political philosophy] of the social contract theory from Hobbes through Locke to Rousseau was widely publicized, and became part of the vocabulary of ordinary political discussion both in Europe and America, as did the concept of 'natural rights.'"

Although Brinton mentions only the sequence Hobbes–Locke–Rousseau, it has often been noticed that the image of a social contract, albeit in a hidden form, also figures in Kant's thought. But—and this is why the charge of "atomistic individualism" has so frequently been brought against social contract theorists—the very picture of a "social contract" assumes that there could *be* fully moral beings, in the Kantian sense of beings who seek to be guided by principles which all similar beings could accept (note that this sense builds in what I have called "reflective transcendence") who still need *reasons* why they should form themselves into a *community*. The human being is conceived of as if she might be a fully constituted intelligent person—and indeed, in the Kantian inflection of the model, a fully constituted *moral* person—*prior to* entering into society. This whole way of thinking was already contested in the nineteenth century, notably by Hegel.

It is perhaps significant that Dewey himself began his

philosophical career as a Hegelian. For Dewey, as for Hegel, we are communal beings from the start. Even as a "thought experiment," the idea that beings who belong to no community could so much as have the idea of a "principle," or a special motive to be guided by principles, is utterly fantastic. On the other hand, unlike empiricist thinkers such as Hume and Bentham, Dewey does not think that a moral community can be constituted merely by the emotion of sympathy. As he writes,

> Sympathy is a genuine natural instinct, varying in intensity in different individuals. It is a precious instrumentality for the development of social insight and socialized affection; *but in and of itself it is on the same plane as any natural endowment.* [emphasis added] It may lead to sentimentality or to selfishness; the individual may shrink from scenes of misery because of the pain they cause him, or may seek jovial companions because of the sympathetic pleasures he gets. Or he may be moved by sympathy to labor for the good of others, but, because of lack of deliberation and thoughtfulness, be quite ignorant of what their good really is, and do a great deal of harm . . . Again instinctive sympathy is partial: it may attach itself to those of blood kin or to immediate associates in such a way as to favor them at the expense of others, and lead to positive injustice to those beyond the charmed circle.[17]

Needless to say, Dewey is not attacking sympathy as such. What he calls for is a *transformation* of sympathy. Like Aristotle, he believes that the reasons for being ethical are not apparent from a non-ethical or pre-ethical standpoint—one must be *educated* into the ethical life, and this education presupposes that one is already *in* a community; it is not something that brings community into existence.

Dewey would agree with Kant that the person whose impulses are transformed in this way, the Deweyan moral person, treats the ends of others as something other than mere means. Her sympathy is not something that *competes with* her other impulses, but something that fuses with them. Such a person thinks in terms of "we" rather than simply "me." Thus she obeys the Kingdom of Ends formulation of Kant's Categorical Imperative (always to regard the humanity in the other as an end, and not merely as a means). But Dewey's account of *moral motivation* is quite different from Kant's. For Kant, it is the "dignity" of obeying "the moral law" that is the motive (which means, ultimately, the "dignity" of giving myself a law that all other rational beings can also give themselves, the dignity of "autonomy"). For Dewey, there is no separate, and certainly no uniquely transcendent, moral motivation that we have to postulate, only our pluralistic and disparate but *morally tranformed* interests and aspirations. The Kantian dualism of "reason" and "inclination" is rejected from the beginning.

The Enlightenment, as already pointed out, taught us to see the *legitimacy* of states as based upon the consent of the governed. Certainly, Dewey (or James, or Mead, or any other of the classical pragmatists) would not wish to challenge the idea that a legitimate state must have the consent of those whom it governs. But the Enlightenment *derived* the idea of the consent of the governed from the model of society as arising from a social contract. In effect, it derived sociability as well as morality from an idealized image of the law of contracts, from *property law.* And Dewey, like Hegel, thinks that this is ridiculous.[18]

In contrast to the entire social contract tradition, Dewey

does not try to justify standing within society (or within the ethical life) at all, and *a fortiori* does not try to justify it either by appeal to a transcendent motive, like Kant, or by appeal to an admittedly fictitious "social contract." For Dewey, the problem is not to justify the existence of communities, or to show that people ought to make the interests of others their own; the problem is to justify the claim that morally decent communities should be *democratically* organized. This Dewey does by appealing to the need to deal intelligently rather than unintelligently with the ethical and practical problems that we confront. Dewey's arguments against the idea that we can simply hand our problems over to experts (there was a famous exchange between Dewey and Lippman on this issue in the 1920s)[19] and his insistence that the most ordinary of individuals has at least one field of unique expertise—if only the knowledge of where his or her "shoe pinches"—are part of what Ruth Anna Putnam and I have called Dewey's "epistemological defense of democracy."[20] Dewey argued that without the participation of the public in the formation of such policy, it could not reflect the common needs and interests of the society because those needs and interests were known only to the public. And those needs and interests cannot be known without democratic "consultation and discussion which uncover social needs and troubles." Hence, Dewey said, "a class of experts is inevitably so removed from common interests as to become a class with private interests and private knowledge, which in social matters is not knowledge at all."

It would be a grave error to read this statement of Dewey's as claiming that experts *inevitably* "become a class with private interests and private knowledge." As Dewey makes clear in many of his essays and books, we *need* experts, including social scientists and professional educators like himself. What he argued against is the view that the role of the ordinary citizens in a democracy should be confined to voting every so many years on the question of which group of experts to appoint. As his own primary contribution to bringing about a different sort of democracy, a "participatory," or better a "deliberative" democracy, he focused his efforts on promoting what was then a new conception of education. If democracy is to be both participatory and deliberative, education must not be a matter of simply teaching people to learn things by rote and believe what they are taught. In a deliberative democracy, learning how to think for oneself, to question, to criticize, is fundamental. But thinking for oneself does not exclude—indeed it requires—learning when and where to seek expert knowledge.

That our communities should be democracies follows, for Dewey, from the fact that only in a democracy does everyone have a chance to make his or her contribution to the discussion; and that they should be *social* democracies follows from the fact that the huge inequalities in wealth and power that we permit to exist effectively block the interests and complaints of the most oppressed from serious consideration, and thus prevent any serious attempt at the solution of such problems as the alleviation of stubborn poverty, or deeply entrenched unemployment, or the inferior educational opportunities afforded to the children most in need of education, from ever getting off the ground.

But there is yet another difference between Dewey and—not just the Enlightenment, but the whole conception of ethics or moral philosophy that dominated and still dominates the thinking of the great majority of philosophers down to the present day. I don't know of any better way to indicate what the received conception is than by quoting a couple of sentences from John Rawls's magnificent lectures on the history of moral philosophy. Very early in that work, in the section titled "The Problem of Modern Moral Philosophy,"[21] we read:

> Here I think of the tradition of moral philosophy as itself a family of traditions, such as the traditions of the natural law and of the moral sense schools and of the traditions of ethical intuitionism and of utilitarianism. What makes all these traditions part of one inclusive tradition is that they use a commonly understood vocabulary and terminology. Moreover, they reply and object to one another's conclusions and arguments, so that exchanges between them are, in part, a reasoned discussion that leads to further development.

In the tradition Rawls describes, and to which he himself has made such a significant contribution, moral philosophy deals with judgments that contain the familiar ethical concepts *right, wrong, just, unjust, good, bad, right, duty, obligation,* and the rest. What is more important, moral philosophy continues to be thought of as a matter of adjudicating between different familiar traditions—today, varieties of Kantianism and Utilitarianism still being at the forefront of the debate—and moral philosophy is still conceived of as involving fairly predictable kinds of arguments containing the familiar handful of abstract ethical terms.

Nothing could be farther from Dewey's conception of ethics. For Dewey, ethics is not a small corner of a professional field called "philosophy," and one cannot assume that its problems can be formulated in any one fixed vocabulary, or illuminated by any fixed collection of "isms." For Dewey, as for James, philosophy is not and should not be primarily a professional discipline, but rather something that all reflective human beings engage in to the extent that they practice "criticism of criticisms." The question of ethics is at least as broad as the question of the relation of philosophy in *this* sense to life. Any human problem at all, insofar as it impacts our collective or individual welfare, is thus far "ethical"—but it may also be at the same time aesthetic, or logical, or scientific, or just about anything else; and if we solve a problem and cannot say, at the end of the day, whether it was an "ethical problem" in the conventional sense of the term, that is not at all a bad thing. Thinking of logic, as Dewey did, as the theory of inquiry and not as a branch of mathematics that happens to be taught in philosophy departments, and of ethics as the relation of inquiry to life—so that the same book, e.g., Dewey's *Logic,* viewed one way is a text in logic (or in epistemology, even if Dewey disliked the word) and viewed another way is a book about social ethics—is, I believe, the right way, indeed the only way, to *open up* the whole topic of ethics, to let the fresh air in. And that is an essential part of what I have been calling "the pragmatist enlightenment" calls for.

In this lecture I have claimed that there have been *learning processes* in history, and that there can be further learning in the future. I have depicted the appearance on the historical stage of the kind of reflection illustrated by the discussion between Socrates and Euthyphro, which I quoted at the start of this lecture, as representing a learning process. I have depicted the eventual rejection of the meritocratic view of the ideal society advocated by Plato as a result not of mere "contingency," but of human experience and of intelligent reflection on that experience. I have depicted the great experiments in democracy which began in the eighteenth century, and the ideas of the Enlightenment, as a further learning process; and I have depicted Dewey's fallibilism and his internal linking of fallibilistic inquiry and democracy, as well as his reconceptualization of ethics as a project of inquiry rather than a set of rules or formulas, as an extension of that learning process.

There are many thinkers to whom my talk of three enlightenments will seem naïve. "Poststructuralists," positivists, and a host of others will react with horror. But I have chosen to speak in this way to make clear that I am an unreconstructed believer in progress, though not, indeed, progress in the stupid sense of a belief that advance either in ethics or in social harmony is inevitable. "Progress" in that sense is just a secular version of eschatology. But what I do believe in is the *possibility* of progress. Such a belief can indeed be abused—what belief can't be? But to abandon the idea of progress and the enterprise of enlightenment—when that abandonment is more than just fashionable "postmodern" posturing—is to trust oneself to the open sea while throwing away the navigation instruments. I hope we shall not be so unwise.

Skepticism about Enlightenment

In the previous lecture I characterized philosophy as an enterprise that aims at what I called "reflective transcendence"—the act of standing back from conventional beliefs,
received opinions, and even received practices, and asking a
penetrating "Why should we accept this as right?"[1] At certain crucial moments in history, the result is a profound
revaluation of our ways of thinking, which we may call "enlightenment." I cited Plato as a philosopher of enlightenment, in this sense, and I used as examples his criticism of
religious fanaticism and his brilliant defense of the proposi-
tion that all offices in society ought to be open to women as
well as men. The second enlightenment, in my list, was the
one best known by that name, the seventeenth- and eighteenth-century movement associated with the names of
Hobbes and Spinoza, Rousseau and Kant, Voltaire and the
philosophes. I characterized that enlightenment as representing a faith in the powers of the new sciences, powers which it
hoped to apply to thinking about social and moral problems, and a conception of society as a social contract. I said

that although we certainly want to retain the idea of the consent of the governed, the second enlightenment had deeply faulty conceptions in many respects. I then described John Dewey's characterization of *both* wings of the Enlightenment, the rationalist wing and the empiricist wing, as deeply aprioristic, albeit in different ways, with the result that their program of thinking "scientifically" about society and man ended, in both cases, in metaphysical fantasies of various sorts. And I argued that the whole program of providing a metaphysical foundation for ethics and for society—for example, providing a reason why we ought to be social beings at all—mislocates the contribution that philosophy can and should make. I suggested that we need a "third enlightenment," one whose conception of knowledge is much more fallibilistic than that of the seventeenth and eighteenth century—fallibilistic and antimetaphysical, but without lapsing into skepticism. I described Dewey as, in many ways, the philosopher who points us in the direction we need for such a third enlightenment.

When I remarked in the previous lecture that my talk of enlightenment might seem naïve to poststructuralists, positivists, and "a host of others," I wanted to make clear that I am a believer in progress, though not in the nineteenth-century sense of inevitable advance in ethics or in social life. What I believe in is the *possibility* of progress. To use a phrase of Habermas's of which Dewey would have approved, I believe that there have been *learning processes* in history, and that there *can* be further learning in the future.

I wish now to consider certain reasons that have been advanced for rejecting the very possibility of learning processes in social history and of rational persuasion in ethics. I shall not attempt to cover *all* the reasons that have been advanced by present-day and past philosophers; that would obviously be too vast an undertaking. In particular, I will not discuss the logical positivist views, which were influential for a large part of the twentieth century in convincing people that there could be no such thing as reasoning about ethical questions;[2] I have discussed these views amply in the past, and have treated them in detail again in a recent book.[3] What I want to consider instead are two very contemporary sorts of reasons for rejecting all talk of "progress," of "learning processes," of "reasoning" in ethics, and the like—one associated with the label "postmodernism" and the other, more broadly, with such labels as "historicism" and "relativism." But my aim will not be simply to "bash" so-called postmodern philosophy. Indeed, there are important things we can learn from the French philosophers—Foucault and Derrida—that I am going to criticize, and there are important analytic philosophers whom I will also criticize—in particular, I will be criticizing the recent writing of Bernard Williams, one of the most brilliant analytic philosophers I know, as well as some of the writing of my friend Richard Rorty, whose work reflects both analytic and "continental" influences, in the course of this lecture. (To tell the truth, I have never thought that classifying philosophy as "analytic" or "continental" is a good thing. But that would be a subject for a different occasion.)

"Postmodern" skepticism about reason-talk has many forms, but I will distinguish only two, one more apparent in the writing of Michel Foucault (although it is also present in Derrida's writing at times) and the other apparent in Derrida.[4] I find Foucault extremely powerful when he analyzes the history of specific institutions, for example, the prison or the clinic. What he does in these philosophical histories of the prison or the clinic is to show us how talk of progress and of reason has been *abused,* how it has served as a rationalization for what he calls the "normalization," that is to say, the bureaucratic administration, of people's lives.

Foucault is unquestionably right that the institution of the prison is not a very good one—and, I might add, especially not as it is used or rather abused in the United States today. However, one should remember that when the philosophers he criticized (e.g., Jeremy Bentham) argued for the "penitentiary" as a form of punishment (and, they hoped, rehabilitation), what they were opposing was, on the one hand, *torture,* and, on the other hand, *capital punishment*— not, indeed, capital punishment as such, but capital punishment for the most trivial thefts, and even for juvenile offenders. When he criticizes the clinic, similarly, Foucault may perhaps be right that there are better methods of treating most patients than the clinic as it has come to be—and its present form does necessarily involve administration by a bureaucracy. Anarchist that he was, however, Foucault felt not the slightest responsibility for explaining in any detail what an *alternative* form of treatment—one that would be available to millions of people in huge societies—could be like, any more than he felt the slightest responsibility to suggest an alternative method of dealing with criminals— something that many people have thought about (perhaps because it is impossible to think of an alternative that wouldn't still involve some degree of bureaucracy). Perhaps Foucault would have rejected the question I just posed; that is, he might have rejected the assumption that we need governments or administrations if we are to have societies with anything like the present number of people, and which live at anything like the present standard of either economic or physical security (bad as that admittedly is, in many places). The problem with "anarchist" critiques in general is that it is all too easy to criticize when you don't accept the responsibility to propose realistic alternatives to the institutions and practices that you criticize.

But Foucault's politics (or lack thereof) aside, his critique does contain important theoretical insights. "Archaeology," in Foucault's sense, is a history of ideas that takes the idea of conceptual structure seriously. To investigate the origins of our penal system, or the clinic, in this way is to look for systems of concepts, systems that have internal logical coherence because some of the concepts depend on others, and especially for systems that determine what Foucault calls an "epistemology"—that is, systems that structure what counts as a problem, what as a possible solution, what as a justification. Although "analytic" philosophers still often write as if concepts were a-historic entities (which is exactly how they were conceived of by the fathers of analytic philosophy, Moore and Russell), there is no reason for their latter-day successors to deny that concepts have a history, and that conceptual analysis and historical analysis can fruitfully enrich each other—and indeed some fine analytic philosophers have been influenced by Foucault to attempt just such a project.[5] What is disturbing about some of Foucault's work—particularly his early work—is that it seems to identify historical analysis of concepts with showing that the evolution of our systems of concepts is simply a matter of power struggles. The very possibility of concepts evolving as a result of what I have been calling *learning processes* seems to be missing in that work (although it is not inconceivable that toward the end of his life Foucault might have been open to it).

In a book I published about twenty years ago *(Reason, Truth, and History)*, I expressed my worry by saying that in Foucault's way of thinking our present beliefs, for example our belief in the clinic as a way of administering medical treatment, are no more rational than the medieval belief in the Divine Right of Kings.[6] My reply to this claim was to say the following: First, belief in the Divine Right of Kings was, in fact, an *irrational* belief even in the Middle Ages. Second, if, indeed, Foucault is right, and our belief that we need clinics—and likewise our belief that we need, if not the penitentiary, then some government-administered way of dealing with criminal offenders—is equally irrational, there is no reason why that could not be *shown.* To be sure, belief in progress has been abused—so, by the way, has the belief that progress is impossible!—it would be hard to find any belief about *anything* that has not been abused in some context or other. But this constitutes a *principled* threat to the power of intelligence to solve problems only if we see it as calling into question the very notion of rationality.

I spelled this out in *Reason, Truth, and History* by saying that it is and always was reasonable to doubt that the Church has privileged access to God's wishes; and if we reject the premise that the Church has privileged access to God's wishes, we will have very good reason to think the Divine Right of Kings was and is an irrational doctrine. I also pointed out that even believing Catholics now concede that the Church's support for monarchy in the Middle Ages was based as much on political considerations as on revelation or sound theology. In short, the belief in the Divine Right of Kings lacks, and, I claim, always lacked, a rational justification.

As I reported in *Reason, Truth, and History*,[7] I showed the pages in which I wrote this to someone who supported Foucault's view, and (I must admit, not to my surprise) my friend was outraged. He argued that *of course* belief in the Divine Right of Kings was "rational," that is, rational *in the Middle Ages*, given what Foucault would call the *jeu de vérité*, the "game of truth," that people played then.

Now, of course there is a *sense* of "rational" in which any view that has a well thought out and intelligent defense on the basis of the shared assumptions of a community can be called "rational," no matter what those shared assumptions might be; but *that* sense is not the normatively important one. To deny that there is a sense of "rational" that goes beyond the sense provided by whatever *jeu de vérité* we happen to be playing at a given moment in history—or to say, as Richard Rorty once did, that "I view warrant as a sociological matter, to be ascertained by observing the reception of S's statement by her peers"[8]—is simply to capitulate to a form of cultural relativism. Cultural relativism is, indeed, an important issue to be faced, and I will turn to it in a little while.

But there is another kind of skepticism to be addressed, a kind that has been made famous by Derrida, which I also want to say something about. Two strains of thought in Derrida (actually, of course, more than two) converge on the idea that there is no getting outside of "texts." (As he puts it, "The problematique of representation has collapsed.")[9] One strain is the idea of a bottomless regress of interpretations.

Deconstructionists claim that all perception and thought involve interpretation, and that every interpretation is susceptible to still further interpretation. Part of this is both true and important. If I see, for example, that a letter is written in blue ink, I employ a concept, the concept *blue ink,* which *could* require interpretation in *some* contexts. To use an example from a recent book by Charles Travis,[10] I go to a stationery store and ask for a bottle of blue ink. I am given a bottle of black liquid. "I asked for blue ink," I protest. "Try it," the clerk tells me. I dip my pen in the black liquid and attempt to write, and to my great surprise I find that the writing is a bright blue! Did the clerk then offer me blue ink? I shall have to think about how I understand "blue ink" then and there.

But this is not a possibility I *always* need to consider when I see that a letter is written in blue ink. Pragmatists say that further interpretation is only required (indeed, a Wittgensteinian would say *only makes sense*)[11] in certain contexts. What deconstructionists do is treat *every* context as a context in which *everything* that is written, said, or thought requires interpretation (and indeed, to the extent that it is understood, is understood by way of interpretation). The only way that deconstructionists envisage of stopping an infinite regress of interpretations would be to claim that there are *self-interpreting* entities—Fregean Thoughts, or "concepts," or Platonic "meanings," or what have you. If one tries, in what I have just suggested is a pragmatist (and also Wittgensteinian) fashion, to distinguish between contexts in which the need for—indeed the very question of—interpretation arises and contexts in which it does not arise at all, deconstructionists are extremely skilled at providing examples of cases in which that distinction cannot be determinately drawn.

About all this, there are at least two things to be said. First, the sheer hubris of supposing that a few philosophical arguments, be they good or bad, of the kind that I have just described can really overthrow the very idea that thought has reference to objects outside of thought and language, or can overthrow the idea that we can speak of the meanings of things that are said and written, or the idea that notions of good and bad argument, that justification and reason and the like make sense—the very idea that all of this can be and has been overthrown by a handful of philosophical arguments seems to me an example of breathtaking arrogance.

I remember once, some years ago, I was having dinner with a group of graduate students at a large Midwestern university, one of whom was an enthusiastic Derridean. At that time, a favorite expression in deconstructionist circles was "ça se met en abîme," *that puts itself in the abyss,* i.e., that deconstructs itself. I asked the young man, "Do you really think that *every* utterance deconstructs itself?" and he said, "Yes." I said, "A minute ago I said, 'Pass the butter.' Did *that* put itself in the abyss?" He paused for a moment—I saw his Adam's apple go up and down as he gulped—and then he bravely said, "*Yes.*"

Although I do not think it is right or fair to criticize Derrida himself for this, many professors nowadays (in the United States they are mostly to be found in literature departments, I have noticed) seem to think that Western logic and Western science were discovered to be unsound in Paris some time after 1960. Indeed, the very idea that there is a world out there was discovered to be unsound in Paris some time after 1960. For it to be even faintly reasonable to think that might be the case (oops! I just said "reasonable," didn't I?), then the arguments in question would have to be better than they are—they would have, at the very least, not to be *obviously* vulnerable to criticism. In fact, both arguments are terribly weak. From the fact that a distinction cannot be drawn in all cases, it does not follow in any way that it is not valid where it can be drawn. To suppose the contrary is as if I were to put someone before you who has fuzz on his head, and we agreed that it was indeterminate whether this person should be called *bald* or *not bald,* and we were then to conclude that we must scrap the distinction between bald and not bald. It is noteworthy that Wittgenstein, whose texts some deconstructionists have lately taken to quoting in support of their views, explicitly attacks the idea that words that are not clearly defined in all cases are worthless. For example, in *Philosophical Investigations* we find:

> §88. If I tell someone "Stand roughly here"—may not this explanation work perfectly? And cannot every other one fail to?

I note, by the way, that in a carefully argued paper Chris Mortensen has criticized in detail Derrida's arguments in his celebrated essay "Plato's Pharmacy and Derrida's Drugstore,"[12] and in particular he has documented Derrida's extensive reliance on precisely the mode of argument I just criticized, a mode of argument which even the normally sympathetic Richard Rorty rejects as depending on the assumption "that unless a distinction can be made rigorous and precise it isn't really a distinction at all." (Rorty is here quoting Searle, who, he says, "is, I think, right.") Rorty also says that many of Derrida's arguments are "awful" (although he characteristically claims that this doesn't really matter very much).[13] Even though the "assumption" Rorty cites is one that Derrida would undoubtedly reject if asked point-blank "Do you believe this?", Mortensen and Rorty are right in thinking that at crucial points Derrida's arguments depend upon it.

The metaphysical idea of a bottomless regress of interpretations which figures in Derrida's writing seems to me even weaker because it ignores two fundamental pragmatist insights, namely: (1) that interpretation is not something that is called for in every case, but only in circumstances where there is doubt as to what a text means or what a person means by her words; and (2) there is neither need for nor possibility of a perfectly precise rule which says which are those circumstances. As Wittgenstein writes:

> §84. I said that the application of a word is not everywhere bounded by rules. For what does a game look like that is everywhere bounded by rules? Whose rules never let a doubt creep in, but stuff up all the cracks where it might?—Can't we imagine a rule determining the application of a rule, and a doubt that it removes—and so on?

And notice how the section continues:

> But that is not to say that we are in doubt because it is possible for us to *imagine* a doubt. I can easily imagine someone always doubting before he opened his front door whether an abyss did not yawn behind it; and making sure about it before he went through the door (and he might on some occasion prove to be right)—but that does not make me doubt in the same case.

In short: we don't need a "rule" to take care of a "doubt" that is wholly without justification!

In spite of such statements on Wittgenstein's part, some deconstructionists nevertheless see his rule-following discussion as *supporting* the regress of interpretations argument; but as Martin Stone has shown, the whole point of Wittgenstein's discussions is precisely to show, to use Wittgenstein's own words in §201, "There is a way of grasping a rule which is *not* an *interpretation,* but which is exhibited in what we call 'obeying the rule' and 'going against it' in actual cases. Hence there is an inclination to say: every action according to the rule is an interpretation. But we ought to restrict the term 'interpretation' to the substitution of one expression of the rule for another." As Stone writes, "The paradoxical regress of interpretation is to be avoided, in Wittgenstein's view, by dropping the assumption that causes all the trouble: namely that one could not follow a rule unless one first attached some interpretation to it."[14]

Although I have been criticizing Derrida—and even more, a certain reception of Derrida—let me emphatically declare that I have no intention of reading him out of the profession of philosophy, in the manner of his more enthusiastic "analytic" opponents. In spite of all the exaggeration and "overkill" I find in his writing, one can still learn from Derrida—certainly, one can learn that the language of enlightenment, the language of reason, even the language of morality should often be distrusted. Derridean critique is *sometimes* in place. The important thing is to perceive *when* a text should be read "deconstructively" and *when* this is not the way a text should be read. We needn't view Derrida as somebody from whom we can't learn anything. But at this time it is important to say that we needn't and we mustn't view Derrida as somebody whose most radical claims have to be believed. And yet world-historical significance has been attached to conclusions reached by arguments this dubious![15] I do not deny for one moment that Derrida is a significant philosopher, but I have to admit that my reaction to the chatter about "postmodernism" as a whole is that it is sad to see so much clamor about stuff so lacking in intellectual substance.

Finally, I turn to cultural relativism. This comes in two versions. The more extreme or "industrial-strength" version is represented by Richard Rorty, and the moderate version is represented by another famous philosopher, Bernard Williams. I will say very little here about Rorty's industrial-strength cultural relativism. (I am aware, of course, that Rorty denies being a cultural relativist, which is why I spoke before of relativism *or* historicism; Rorty's position, in the terminology of one of my critical essays long ago,[16] is properly described as a form of cultural *imperialism* rather than cultural relativism; however, with respect to the concept of *justification* he is an explicit relativist.) Although with respect to *truth*, Rorty's position is that what is true and false is determined by the norms of "our" ("wet liberal") culture, he is willing to say that what is *justified* to believe in other cultures is decided by the sociological facts about those cultures. By using here the phrase "sociological fact" in explaining Rorty's position, I have flagged one of the respects in which I think his view is self-refuting: I think that Rorty's position presupposes a naïve realism about sociological facts, norms of "our" culture, etc., which is contrary to the position as a whole. (For those who are interested in the details, I recommend the exchange between us in the recently published Festschrift for Rorty edited by Robert Brandom.)[17]

Bernard Williams's latest statement of his views is set out in a lecture replying to some of my own criticisms recently published in the British journal *Philosophy*.[18] This essay is titled "Philosophy as a Humanistic Discipline," and it reflects throughout the same concern with achieving a reflective understanding of the history of the subject that lay behind my previous lecture. It clearly aspires both to praise and to exhibit what I have called "reflective transcendence"; and certainly Williams does not believe that justification is just "a sociological matter, to be ascertained by observing the reception of S's statement by her peers," as Rorty does. The sciences, in particular, Williams sees as converging to what he calls an "absolute" conception of the world, a conception which reveals (to the maximum extent possible) how things are in themselves, independently of human "perspectives." This makes it all the more sad that when it comes to just the issues that I have been discussing here, we find him driven to views surprisingly similar in certain respects to Rorty's. Here is the background:

Bernard Williams, as I do, thinks that it is important to reflect on what he calls "a historical story of how these concepts rather than others came to be ours."[19] Let us look at the passage:

> If we ask why we use some concepts of this [political and ethical] kind rather than others—rather than, say, those current in an earlier time—we may deploy arguments which claim to justify our ideas against those others; ideas of equality and

equal rights, for instance, against ideas of hierarchy. Alternatively, we may reflect on an historical story, of how these concepts rather than others came to be ours: a story (simply to give it a label) of how the modern world and its special expectations came to replace the *ancien régime.* But then we reflect on the relation of this story to the arguments that we deploy against the earlier conceptions, and we realize that the story is the history of those forms of argument themselves: the forms of argument, call them liberal forms of argument, are a central part of the outlook that we accept.

If we consider how these forms of argument came to prevail, we can indeed see them as having won, but not necessarily as having won an argument. For liberal ideas to have won an argument, the representatives of the *ancien régime* would have had to have shared with the nascent liberals a conception of something that the argument was about, and not just in the obvious sense that it was about the way to live or the way to order society. They would have had to agree that there was some aim, of reason or freedom or whatever, which liberal ideas served better or of which they were a better expression, and there is not much reason, with a change as radical as this, to think that they did agree about this, at least until late in the process. The relevant ideas of freedom, reason, and so on were themselves involved in the change. If in this sense the liberals did not win an argument, then the explanations of how liberalism came to prevail—that is to say, among other things, how these came to be our ideas—are not vindicatory.[20]

Contrast this pessimistic appraisal of the possibility of giving what Williams calls a "vindicatory" history of the evolution of the liberal outlook (of what I called in the previous lecture the second and third enlightenments) with his optimistic view of the possibility of giving a vindicatory history of scientific discovery, expressed a couple of pages earlier:[21]

> There is of course a real question of what it is for a history to be a history of discovery. One condition of its being so lies in a familiar idea, which I would put like this: the later theory, or (more generally) outlook, makes sense of itself, and of the earlier outlook, and of the transition from the earlier to the later, in such terms that both parties (the holders of the earlier outlook, and the holders of the later) have reason to recognize the transition as an improvement. I shall call an explanation which satisfies this condition *vindicatory*. In the particular case of the natural sciences, the later theory typically explains in its own terms the appearances which supported the earlier theory, and, furthermore, the earlier theory can be understood as a special or limited case of the former.[22]

Williams here isn't simply defining a technical term ("vindicatory"), whose meaning he is free to stipulate as he pleases. What he is offering is an account of *rational justification*, and it is clear that the only alternative he sees to a "vindicatory" account of how we came to believe something is an account which simply gives up the idea that changing our beliefs was a learning process at all. We see this, for example, when he says that "we *must* attend [to the question of the existence of a vindicatory history] if we are to know what reflective attitude to take to our own conceptions."[23] The passage continues:

> For one thing the answer to the question whether there is a history of our conceptions that is vindicatory (if only modestly so) makes a difference to what we are doing in saying, if we do say, that the earlier conceptions were wrong. In the absence of vindicatory explanations, while you can of course say that they were wrong—who is to stop you?—the content

of this is likely to be pretty thin. It conveys only the message that the earlier outlook fails by arguments the point of which is that such outlooks should fail by them. It is a good question whether a tune as thin as this is worth whistling at all.

So the real question is whether one *can* see the development of enlightenment as a learning process, and Williams is quite right to say, as he does two pages later,

> To some extent this is one version of a problem that has recurred in European thought since historical self-consciousness struck deep roots in the early nineteenth century: a problem of reflection and commitment, or of an external view of one's beliefs as opposed to an internal involvement with them—a problem, as it might be called, of historicist weariness and alienation.[24]

In order to bring the issue down to earth, let us consider again the example I used a little while ago, namely our coming to see the arguments for the Divine Right of Kings as bad arguments. The medieval Church defended the Divine Right of Kings with an appeal—an appeal in which, I think, any good Talmudist would have had no difficulty in exposing all kinds of holes—to the story in the Bible of how God (reluctantly and angrily!) conceded to the Israelites' wish to have a king (so that they could be like the other nations!). Now, it is essential to the outlook of all three enlightenments that although an enlightened person can certainly be religious, an enlightened person does not take every sentence of the Bible (or, in Plato's case, of Greek mythology) as authoritative on either cosmological or political matters. (Indeed, the rabbis of the Talmud were already enlightened in this sense.)[25] Moreover—and this is the beginning of what I called the "pragmatist enlightenment"—enlightened persons no longer take the opinions of philosophers who claim to have "apriori proofs" concerning matters of fact or of politics as authoritative. As Peirce put it, in his great essay "The Fixation of Belief," we have learned that the Method of Authority and the Method of What is Agreeable to Reason are bad ways of fixing belief. And Peirce was quite willing to describe this discovery as "in Bacon's phrase, a true induction,"[26] that is to say, an illustration of the very scientific method we have come to valorize. For pragmatists, the rejection of every form of fundamentalism and the rejection of every form of apriorism are essential to a proper understanding of what a learning process *is*.

Now let us recall Williams's words that I quoted earlier: "For liberal ideas to have won an argument, the representatives of the *ancien régime* would have had to have shared with the nascent liberals a conception of something that the argument was about, and not just in the obvious sense that it was about the way to live or the way to order society." Williams then identified what they would have had to agree on, namely, "that there was some aim, of reason or freedom or whatever, which liberal ideas served better or of which they were a better expression," and he added "and there is not much reason, with a change as radical as this, to think that they did agree about this, at least until late in the process." But this is stacking the cards with a vengeance!

Rather than it being the case that people *started* with ideas like "freedom" (in the modern sense), or "reason" (in the modern sense), and then moved *from* those principles to the rejection of the Divine Right of Kings, there is every reason to think the reverse; that is, to say that people perceived that reliance on the Bible, as interpreted by the Church, with respect to astronomical matters was a bad idea (in part because the new astronomy was slowly but surely producing results which—as Galileo showed—were difficult to square with Ptolemaic astronomy, which was the astronomy that the Church accepted because it preserved what the Church saw as essential parts of the biblical description). In addition, the Catholic Church had exploited its privileged right to say what the proper interpretation of the Bible was supposed to be to such an extent as to produce a many-sided reaction, the reaction we know as Protestantism. Once people were allowed (or allowed themselves the freedom) to discuss alternative understandings of the Bible, the whole idea that the Bible in any way obviously and clearly mandates that every society must have a king, or that if a society does have a king, then that king rules by Divine Right, was seen to be extremely dubious. It is *after* the Divine Right of Kings has been questioned, that is, when people have already begun to search for alternative conceptions "about the way to live or the way to order society," that modern ideas of freedom and reason arise as people begin to formulate the conceptions which will guide them when they live in societies which no longer have absolute monarchs—and, of course, once monarchy came into question, then aristocracy was soon likewise questioned.

Williams gives great weight to the thought that such arguments and conceptions would not have convinced "representatives of the *ancien régime*." But neither did they convince representatives of the Church in the case of Galileo! What really leads Williams astray, I think, is his too limited conception of the choice we face. Williams's choice is simply to see what I have called the Enlightenment (and what I have called the "pragmatist enlightenment" as well, to the extent that it prevails) as simply "contingent," a notion that Rorty too exploits,[27] which is why Williams thinks it necessary to distinguish himself from Rorty by rejecting Rorty's valorization of "irony." Thus Williams writes,

> In fact, as it seems to me, once one goes *far enough* in recognizing contingency, the problem to which irony is supposed to provide the answer does not arise at all. . . . The supposed problem comes for the idea that a vindicatory history of our outlook is what we would really like to have, and the discovery that liberalism, in particular (but the same is true of any outlook), has the kind of contingent history that it does have is a disappointment, which leaves us with at best a second best. But, once again, why should we think that? Precisely because we are not unencumbered intelligences selecting in principle among all possible outlooks, we can accept that this outlook is ours just because of the history that has made it ours; or, more precisely, has both made us, and made the outlook as something that is ours. We are no less contingently formed than the outlook is, and the formation is significantly the same. We and our outlook are not simply in the same place at the same time. If we really understand this, deeply understand it, we can be free of what is indeed another scientistic illusion, that it is our job as rational agents to search for, or at least move as best we can towards, a system of political and ethical ideas which would be the best from an absolute point of view, a point of view that was free of contingent historical perspective.[28]

Williams sees only two possible positions: *either* the position that he defends, which is to see what I have called "enlightenment" (and what he calls "liberal") values as *merely* "contingent" products of a particular history, but to celebrate the supposed fact that since we are equally "contingent," and we and those values are made for each other, there is no problem (for us) in accepting them (a position which Rorty also espouses in many places[29]—"irony" is not at all times Rorty's stance) *or,* on the other hand, a position which would indeed be "scientistic," namely the position that we can search for, and that it is "our job as rational agents to search for, or at least move as best we can towards, a system of political and ethical ideas which would be the best from an absolute point of view, a point of view that was free of contingent historical perspective." What is missing in this dichotomy is precisely the idea that characterizes my pragmatist "enlightenment": the idea that there is such a thing as the *situated* resolution of political and ethical problems and conflicts (of what Dewey calls "problematical situations"), and that claims concerning evaluations of—and proposals for the resolution of—problematical situations can be more and less *warranted* without being *absolute.* Situated resolutions of problems always require ideas; but they do not require ideas which are "free of contingent historical perspective." Dewey stressed that problematical situations are contingent and their resolutions are likewise contingent; but there is still a difference, an all-important difference, between *thinking* that a claim concerning the resolution of a situation is a warranted claim and its actually *being* warranted. What is missing in Williams's entire discussion is the possibility of a view like Dewey's. What is missing is the very possibility of pragmatism.

Notes / Index

Notes

Introduction

1. For a detailed explanation and defense of this claim about Kant, see Juliet Floyd, "Heautonomy: Kant on Reflective Judgment and Systematicity," in *Kants Ästhetik. Kant's Aesthetics. L'esthétique de Kant,* ed. Herman Parret (Berlin and New York: de Gruyter, 1998).

2. Ludwig Wittgenstein, *Remarks on the Foundations of Mathematics,* ed. G. H. von Wright, R. Rhees, and G. E. M. Anscombe (Oxford: Basil Blackwell, 1956), p. 84, §46: "I should like to say, mathematics is a MOTLEY of techniques of proof" (caps in original).

3. For details, see my *The Collapse of the Fact/Value Dichotomy* (Cambridge, Mass.: Harvard University Press, 2002), especially the first two chapters.

4. John Stuart Mill, *A System of Logic, Ratiocinative and Inductive* [1843] (Toronto: University of Toronto Press, 1973).

5. For a discussion of Dewey's *Logic* and its relation to Mill's *A System of Logic,* see Hilary Putnam and Ruth Anna Putnam, "Dewey's *Logic:* Epistemology as Hypothesis," collected in my *Words and Life,* ed. James Conant (Cambridge, Mass.: Harvard University Press, 1994), pp. 198–220.

6. As charged by, for example, Stanley Cavell in "What's the Use of Calling Emerson a Pragmatist?" in *The Revival of Pragmatism,* ed. Morris Dickstein (Durham, N.C.: Duke University Press, 1998). The most objectionable statement about Dewey, in an essay I find

uncharacteristically insensitive for Cavell, is this one (on p. 79): "But what Dewey calls for other disciplines can do as well, maybe better, than philosophy."

7. Dewey preferred to call himself a student of "the theory of inquiry"; to him the term "epistemology" suggested too much the whole problematic of Cartesian skepticism. Nevertheless, Ruth Anna Putnam and I consider him one of the most important epistemologists of the twentieth century (see "Dewey's *Logic*").

8. Coauthored with James H. Tufts. The whole book is republished as volume 5 of *The Middle Works of John Dewey*, ed. Jo Ann Boydston (Carbondale, Ill.: Southern Illinois University Press, 1978). When I speak of Dewey's vision of human nature in the 1908 edition, I am referring to Part II, "Theory of the Moral Life," written by Dewey.

9. In contemporary moral philosophy, something of this idea can be found, albeit in a more naturalistic form, in the (different) moral theories of Barbara Herman, Christine Korsgaard, and Thomas Scanlon.

10. Dewey, *Ethics*, 1908 edition (see note 8), p. 272.

11. Ibid., p. 273.

12. In his third Critique, *The Critique of Judgment*, Kant himself speaks of the need to overcome this dualism (but leaves it mysterious how this overcoming is to be accomplished).

13. Dewey, *Ethics*, 1908 edition, p. 273.

14. Ibid., pp. 283–284.

15. Ibid., p. 371.

16. I recently heard Herbert Kelman describe himself in this way; I have borrowed the term, because it so perfectly describes Dewey.

NOTES TO PART I

1. Ethics without Metaphysics

1. This is something that those of my readers who have read another set of lectures I gave in Italy almost a decade ago, and published as *Pragmatism: An Open Question* (Oxford: Blackwell, 1995), already know.

2. See my "Rethinking Mathematical Necessity," in *Words and Life,* ed. James Conant (Cambridge, Mass.: Harvard University Press, 1994), pp. 245–263.

3. For a different (and very interesting) interpretation of Plato on Forms, see Antonia Soulez, *La grammaire philosophique chez Platon* (Paris: Presses Universitaires de France, 1991). Soulez's book was called to my attention by reading Jean-Phillippe Narboux's unpublished paper, "Wittgenstein and Plato: Idioms of Paradigms." Narboux also cites Gilbert Ryle's controversial "Letters and Syllables in Plato," in Ryle's *Collected Papers,* vol. 1 (New York: Barnes and Noble, 1971), pp. 54–71. More recently, I encountered a still different interpretation of Plato's transcendentalism in Myles Burnyeat's brilliant lecture, "Plato," *Proceedings of the British Academy* 111, *2000 Lectures and Memoirs* (Oxford: Oxford University Press, 2001).

4. *Nicomachean Ethics,* book I, chapter 6.

5. This was the view of J. L. Mackie in *Ethics: Inventing Right and Wrong* (Harmondsworth: Penguin Books, 1978).

6. Simon Blackburn's "quasi-realism" with respect to mathematics seems to me to be a form of this eliminationist position. See his *Spreading the Word; Groundings in the Philosophy of Language* (Oxford: Clarendon Press, 1984).

7. Wittgenstein, *Philosophical Investigations* (Oxford: Blackwell, 1953), §88.

8. In this connection, see Levinas's *Otherwise than Being; or Beyond Essence,* trans. Alphonso Lingis (Dordrecht: Kluwer, 1991), and also the short essay "Ethics as First Philosophy," collected in *The Levinas Reader,* ed. Sean Hand (Oxford: Oxford University Press, 1989).

9. For an explanation and discussion of this idea, see my "Levinas and Judaism," in Robert Bernasconi and Simon Critchley, eds., *The Cambridge Companion to Levinas* (Cambridge: Cambridge University Press, 2003).

10. On this, see my *The Many Faces of Realism* (LaSalle, Ill.: Open Court, 1987).

11. Which does not mean, the Sages of the Talmud are careful to point out, that we are all the same. As this is expressed in the Bab-

ylonian Talmud, *Sanhedrin* 37a, "When a human being mints a number of coins using one stamp, all of them are similar, one to the other; whereas when the King of Kings, Blessed be He, imprinted every human with His stamp not one of them was like his fellow."

12. In the *Analects* Confucius says (VII, 30): "Is benevolence [or "humanity"] really far away? No sooner do I desire it than it is here." Similarly, Mencius (quoted by Tu Weiming in *Confucian Thought: Selfhood as Creative Transformation* [New York: SUNY Press, 1985], p. 61) states that "For a man to give full realization to his heart is for him to understand his own nature, and a man who knows his own nature will know Heaven." (This is to be read in the light of the accompanying instruction that the way to be "true to myself" is as follows: "Try your best to treat others as you wish to be treated yourself and you will find that this is the shortest way to humanity.") In neither of these thinkers is there any suggestion that only an elite is capable of this "creative transformation," as Tu Weiming calls it. Likewise Zhou Dunyi, in *Tongshu* (chapter 20, "Sagely Study"): writes, "If I was asked: sagehood, can it be studied? I'd say: Yes!" (unpublished translation by Gallia Patt-Shamir). At the same time, however, Confucius tells us (*Analects,* VII, 26): "I have no hope of meeting a sage." There is a fine discussion of the paradoxical coexistence of these two sorts of statements in Gallia Patt-Shamir, "The Riddle of Confucianism: The Case of Tongshu" (doctoral dissertation, Harvard University, 1997).

13. See Nussbaum's *Cultivating Humanity* (Cambridge, Mass.: Harvard University Press, 1997).

14. *Nicomachean Ethics,* Book I, chapter 7.

15. See chapter 7, "Values and Norms," of my *The Collapse of the Fact/Value Dichotomy and Other Essays* (Cambridge, Mass.: Harvard University Press, 2002).

16. Virtually all of Dewey's writings concern ethics in one way or another. In connection with the aspect I am stressing here, see *The Quest for Certainty,* vol. 4 in Jo Ann Boydston, ed., *The Later Works of John Dewey* (Carbondale, Ill.: University of Southern Illinois Press, 1981–1990); *Reconstruction in Philosophy,* included in vol. 12, in Jo Ann Boydston, ed., *The Middle Works of John*

Dewey (Carbondale, Ill.: University of Southern Illinois Press, 1976–1983); *Ethics,* vol. 7 in *The Later Works of John Dewey;* and *Human Nature and Conduct,* vol. 14 in *The Middle Works of John Dewey.*

17. *The Essential Writings of John Dewey,* ed. David Sidorski (New York: Harper Torchbooks, 1977), p. 94. This quotation is from "The Need for a Reform of Philosophy" in *Creative Intelligence: Essays in the Pragmatic Attitude* by John Dewey and others (New York: Henry Holt, 1917; reprinted, New York: Octagon Books, 1970).

18. See Hilary Putnam and Ruth Anna Putnam, "Dewey's *Logic:* Epistemology as Hypothesis," collected in *Words and Life,* ed. Conant, pp. 198–220.

2. A Defense of Conceptual Relativity

1. But see "Vagueness and Alternative Logic," in my *Philosophical Papers,* vol. 3, *Realism and Reason* (Cambridge: Cambridge University Press, 1983), pp. 271–286.

2. Cf. the Third Logical Investigation in Edmund Husserl, *Logical Investigations,* trans. J. N. Findlay (London and New York: Routledge, 2001).

3. See my *The Many Faces of Realism* (LaSalle, Ill.: Open Court, 1987), 16ff.

4. Although in "free logic" this law is not taken to be a logical law.

5. Lecture II of my *The Many Faces of Realism,* p. 18, uses a similar example.

6. Of course, Carnap would not have *objected* to the use of Lezniewski's calculus of parts and wholes; his attitude to such questions was the one I recommend here, that this is a question of the adoption of a convention, and not a question of fact. Unfortunately, Carnap regarded *too many* questions as questions of convention, and this served (unfortunately, in my view) to discredit the idea that *anything* is a matter of convention.

7. It will, in general, turn out to have other parts as well, using the definition of "part of" specified in note 8.

8. If we were to treat them as logical constructions, we could first

define an equivalence relation over sets of individuals, by saying that two sets of individuals are equivalent if the geometrical sums of the regions occupied by the individuals in the first set is the same as the sum of the regions occupied by the individuals in the second set. Having done that, we explain that in translating the Polish Logician's language into a language that we Carnapians understand, what we do is treat quantifications over individuals in that language as quantifications over individuals and sets of individuals (in the Carnapian language), and then interpret "$x = y$" as x is equivalent to y, if x and y are sets, as x is equivalent to the unit set of y, if x is a set and y is an individual, as the unit set of x is equivalent to y, if y is a set and x is an individual, and as identity if x and y are both individuals. Note that every individual is identified with its unit set, by this definition. Finally, "x is a part of y" is defined to mean that the set equivalent to or identical with x is a subset of the set equivalent to or identical with y.

9. Such a philosopher is Trenton Merricks, in *Objects and Persons* (Oxford: Clarendon Press, 2002).

10. Although no contemporary philosopher takes this position (as far as I know), Gideon Rosen and Cian Dorr come close! (in their on-line publication "Composition as a Fiction," available at *http://dorr.philosophy.fas.nyu.edu/*). They write, ". . . for certain philosophical purposes, it may turn out to matter whether composite things in fact exist. It is plausible, however, that at present no such considerations decide the question" (p. 32). They recommend "fictionalist agnosticism."

11. Jennifer Case, "On the Right Idea of a Conceptual Scheme," *Southern Journal of Philosophy*, 35, no. 1 (1997), pp. 1–18.

12. See note 8 for details.

13. See W. V. Quine, "Truth by Convention," collected in his *The Ways of Paradox and Other Essays* (New York: Random House, 1966); and "Carnap and Logical Truth," in P. A. Schilpp, ed., *The Philosophy of Rudolf Carnap* (LaSalle, Ill.: Open Court, 1963), p. 405.

14. David Lewis, *Convention* (Cambridge, Mass.: Harvard University Press, 1969).

15. "Carnap and Logical Truth," in *The Philosophy of Rudolf Carnap*, p. 405.

16. See my "Convention: A Theme in Philosophy," in *Philosophical Papers,* vol. 3, p. 178.

17. See, for example, my "Reply to Jennifer Case" in *Revue Internationale de Philosophie,* 55, no. 4 (2001), pp. 431–438.

18. As suggested by Jennifer Case, "On the Right Idea of a Conceptual Scheme," pp. 1–18.

19. For a more precise definition of the kind of equivalence involved, see "Equivalence" in my *Philosophical Papers,* vol. 3, *Realism and Reason,* pp. 26–45.

20. Not only is such a definition impossible in practice, it would violate the linguistic character of words like "desk" and "table" (cf. Wittgenstein, *Philosophical Investigations,* §75 and §76).

21. However, it was still true in the last half of the twentieth century that some primitive cultures existed in the Amazon that had never heard of such things as tables, chairs, or even clothing.

22. Benjamin Lee Whorf, *Language, Thought, and Reality: Selected Essays of Benjamin Lee Whorf,* ed. John B. Carroll (Cambridge, Mass.: MIT Press, 1956).

23. In "The Very Idea of a Conceptual Scheme," collected in his *Inquiries into Truth and Interpretation* (Oxford: Clarendon Press, 1984), pp. 183–198, Davidson criticizes Whorf without deigning to consider Whorf's examples.

3. Objectivity without Objects

1. For example, the supposition that all properties can be classified into "simple" and "complex," where the criterion is whether our notion of the property is conceptually analyzable or not. A concept which is analyzable in terms of concepts which do not presuppose it is "complex," in Moore's sense, and a "simple" property is one which is not complex. By that criterion, "energy" would be a simple property, since the definition of energy in terms of simpler properties is certainly not a mere conceptual analysis! But energy is reducible, not irreducible, although the reduction is an empirical discovery and not a piece of conceptual analysis.

2. James Conant, "Wittgenstein's Philosophy of Mathematics," *Proceedings of the Aristotelian Society,* vol. 97, part II (1997), pp. 195–222.

3. Sabina Lovibond, *Realism and Imagination in Ethics* (Oxford: Blackwell, 1983), p. 36.

4. Ibid., p. 26.

5. Simon Blackburn, "Review of Paul Johnston, *Wittgenstein on Moral Philosophy*," in *Ethics,* April 1993, p. 589.

6. Ibid., p. 589.

7. Conant, "Wittgenstein's Philosophy of Mathematics," p. 202. I number these two views of Blackburn's (1) and (2) because Conant does so in his paper.

8. See my "On Wittgenstein's Philosophy of Mathematics," *The Aristotelian Society,* Supplementary volume 70 (1996), pp. 243–264.

9. "Was Wittgenstein *Really* an Antirealist about Mathematics?", in Timothy G. McCarthy and Sean Stidd, eds., *Wittgenstein in America* (Oxford: Clarendon Press, 2001).

10. Those philosophers who *do* think it right to reify "statements" (or "propositions") often think of them as immaterial counterparts of sentences which differ from what are colloquially called "statements" in not being susceptible of different interpretations. They often hold that these supposed immaterial objects are the "meanings" of the sentences we utter. This is a way of thinking that Wittgenstein attacked in a conversation with G. E. Moore that Charles Travis discusses at length in *Unshadowed Thought* (Cambridge, Mass.: Harvard University Press, 2000).

11. Sentences are also often identified with integers in formal work, via the device called "Gödel numbering," and inferences with sequences of integers.

12. "$p \supset p \vee q$" is read "If p then p or q."

13. As I have shown in detail in "A Comparison of Something with Something Else," the Tarski procedure ignores rather than explicating the meaning of the word "true." What Tarski did do—and what is enormously useful in mathematical logic—is capture the denotation of that word in particular cases, but not its meaning.

14. If "L" occurred as either a genuine constant or a genuine variable in "true-in-L", then it would have to appear in the *definiens* and not only in the *definiendum,* and a glance at a Tarskian truth-definition will show that it doesn't! Thus it is quite wrong to claim, as Donald Davidson has, that Tarskian truth-definitions capture

the way in which truth is *relative to* or *depends upon* both the sentence in question and upon the language L. Here Davidson is thinking of "S is true-in-L" as a two-place predicate, with variables for both S and L, rather than as a one-place predicate with an argument-place only for a sentence S. But this is precisely the mistake I am pointing out.

15. See sections IV and V (pp. 299–305) in my "Pragmatism," *Proceedings of the Aristotelian Society,* vol. 95, part III (1995), pp. 291–306. In "Rethinking Mathematical Necessity," I referred to them as "statements whose negations we do not (presently) understand." The latter essay is collected in my *Words and Life* (Cambridge, Mass.: Harvard University Press, 1994). The phrase in question occurs on p. 256.

16. Although Quine's reading of Carnap has sometimes been questioned, I think Quine was right to this extent: on Carnap's view, if one ever gives up an analytic truth, one has *ipso facto* changed the meanings of one's words. As long as one understands the meanings of one's words (something that Carnap took to be unproblematic, a matter of knowing rules accepted by a particular scientific community), then one cannot give up any analytic truth.

17. An exceptionally clear statement of the idealist position can be found in Daniel S. Robinson, ed., *Royce's Logical Essays* (Dubuque, Iowa: Wm. C. Brown, 1951). See especially Chapter 5, "Axiom," and the discussion of interpretation on pp. 151ff.

18. I discussed this example in a paper I wrote more than forty years ago, "It Ain't Necessarily So," collected in my *Philosophical Papers,* vol. 1, *Mathematics, Matter, and Method.*

19. W. V. Quine, *Word and Object* (Cambridge, Mass.: MIT Press, 1960), p. 55 and pp. 65–69.

20. Not that one should accept this use of "psychological" as a wastebasket category!

21. *On Certainty,* §248: "I have arrived at the rock bottom of my convictions. And one might almost say that these foundation walls are carried by the whole house."

22. Most recently in "Was Wittgenstein *Really* an Antirealist About Mathematics?", in McCarthy and Stidd, eds., *Wittgenstein in America,* but the germ of the argument is already in two pages (pp. 74–

75) of "Mathematical Truth," collected in *Mathematics, Matter, and Method.* See also pp. 337ff. in the same volume, from an essay (actually a monograph) published in 1971.

23. See Simon Blackburn, *Essays in Quasi-Realism* (Oxford: Oxford University Press, 1993).

24. Identifying sets with (two-valued) functions is a common practice in certain parts of mathematical logic (especially when techniques from recursion theory, including recursion on higher type objects or on ordinals, are used in conjunction with techniques from set theory).

25. A classic introduction to the philosophical problems in this area is Paul Benacerraf's "What Numbers Could Not Be," in P. Benacerraf and H. Putnam, eds., *Philosophy of Mathematics: Selected Readings* (Cambridge: Cambridge University Press, 1964), pp. 272–294.

26. This is the heart of the "modal logical" interpretation of mathematics. It was first proposed in my "Mathematics without Foundations," *Journal of Philosophy,* 64 (1967), pp. 5–22, reprinted in *Mathematics, Matter, and Method,* pp. 60–78. Constructions which carry out the translation of mathematical statements into a modal language that I sketched in that paper have been worked out in detail by others, most notably by Geoffrey Hellman in *Mathematics without Numbers* (Oxford: Clarendon Press, 1989).

27. Or perhaps my memory is playing tricks on me! In Kreisel's review, "Wittgenstein's Remarks on the Foundations of Mathematics," *British Journal for the Philosophy of Science,* 9 (1959), pp. 135–158, footnote 1 on p. 138 does includes the remark that "it should be noted that Wittgenstein argues against the notion of a mathematical object . . . but, at least in places (p. 124, 35, p. 96, 71, lines 5 and 4 from below) not against the objectivity of mathematics especially through his recognition of formal facts (p. 128, 50)." But I still have the feeling that I heard Kreisel say this about Frege.

28. The refutation of Whitehead's theory was the work of C. M. Will, "Relativistic Gravity in the Solar System, II: Anisotrophy in the Newtonian Gravitational Constant," *Astrophysics Journal,* 169 (1971), pp. 409, 412.

4. "Ontology": An Obituary

1. In his "Putnam and the Relativist Menace," *Journal of Philosophy*, 90, no. 9 (September 1993), pp. 443–461, Rorty writes, "I view warrant as a sociological matter, to be ascertained by observing the reception of S's statement by her peers." I reply to this essay in "Richard Rorty on Reality and Justification," in Robert B. Brandom, ed., *Rorty and His Critics* (Oxford: Blackwell, 2000), pp. 81–86.

2. It might be thought that the "reliabilist" epistemology proposed by Alvin Goldman in *Epistemology and Cognition* (Cambridge, Mass.: Harvard University Press, 1986), is a way out. According to that epistemology, what makes a belief in science justified is that its acceptance was arrived at by a method which is "reliable" in the sense of having a high probability of resulting in the acceptance of true hypotheses. To see why this does not succeed, simply consider the question: "On what 'method' was Einstein relying when he accepted the Special and General Theories of Relativity?" Einstein's own views are well known. He tells us that he arrived at the Special Theory of Relativity by *applying an empiricist critique to the notion of "simultaneity"* and that he arrived at General Relativity by *seeking the "simplest" theory of gravity compatible with Special Relativity in the infinitesimal domain.* We know that the physicists who accepted these two theories also regarded these as compelling considerations in their favor. Both of these "methods" are *completely topic-specific* (so much so, that the reference class of theories involved is much too small for it to make sense to speak of "probabilities" here at all!), and both of these methods presuppose judgments of reasonableness. And judgments of reasonableness simply do not fall into classes to which we are able to assign probabilities. (Moreover, any scientific judgment can be regarded as having been arrived at by a virtually infinity of different "methods." "Reliabilism" only *pretends* not to presuppose the notion of reasonableness.)

3. Here I am adapting Kreisel's remark about Frege's philosophy of mathematics.

4. I defend this claim in "Pragmatism and Moral Objectivity," collected in my *Words and Life* (Cambridge, Mass.: Harvard University Press, 1994).

5. I first saw this point in Vivian Walsh, *Scarcity and Evil* (Englewood Cliffs, N.J.: Prentice-Hall, 1961).

6. As Iris Murdoch points out in *The Sovereignty of Good* (New York: Schocken Books, 1971). Besides the American pragmatists, other philosophers who have effectively combated this form of blindness in their writings include Cora Diamond and Rush Rhees.

7. As I pointed out in the first lecture, the latter is the focus of Dewey's writings; not that Dewey underestimated the importance of abstract and universal principles, but that he saw them as *guides*—and fallible guides at that—to the *solution* of practical problems.

8. See my *The Collapse of the Fact/Value Dichotomy* (Cambridge, Mass.: Harvard University Press, 2002).

9. For a profound critique of talk of "in principle irresolvable" moral disputes, see Michele Moody-Adams, *Fieldwork in Familiar Places: Morality, Culture, and Philosophy* (Cambridge, Mass.: Harvard University Press, 1997).

10. "On What There Is," published with revisions in Quine's *From a Logical Point of View* (Cambridge, Mass.: Harvard University Press, 1953, 1960). (Originally published in *The Review of Metaphysics,* 1948.)

11. Quine referred, for example, to the medieval controversies between Nominalists, Conceptualists, and Realists about the existence of classes.

12. "Wyman [an imaginary philosopher], in an ill-conceived attempt to appear agreeable, genially grants us the nonexistence of Pegasus, and then, contrary to what *we* mean by nonexistence of Pegasus, insists that Pegasus *is*. The only way I know of coping with this obfuscation of issues is to *give* Wyman the word 'exist.' I'll try not to use it again; I still have 'is.'" (*From a Logical Point of View,* p. 3. Note Quine's confident appeal to "what we *mean*" in 1948.)

13. Quine, *Theories and Things* (Cambridge, Mass.: Harvard University Press, 1990), p. 100.

14. "Gibson points out a startling contradiction between consecutive essays in *Theories and Things.* There was an appreciable lapse of time in my writing of the two essays, and the more so in that the first one developed from still earlier lectures. I was aware of my change in attitude, but not of so abrupt a conflict." "Reply to Roger

Gibson," in *The Philosophy of W. V. Quine* (LaSalle, Ill.: Open Court, 1986), p. 156. Edward Becker has pointed out (private communication) that Quine continued to vacillate on this issue after the "Reply to Gibson," and has discerned no fewer than seven different positions that Quine took on this issue at different times.

15. Quine, "Reply to Charles Parsons," in L. E. Hahn and P. A. Schilpp, eds., *The Philosophy of W. V. Quine* (Carbondale: University of Southern Illinois Press, 1986), p. 397.

16. "Propositional and attributary attitudes belong to the daily discourse of hopes, fears, and purposes; causal science gets on well without them . . . a reasonable if less ambitious alternative [to attempting to make them "science worthy"] would be to keep a relatively simple and austere conceptual scheme, free of half-entities [*sic*] for official scientific business and then accommodate the half-entities in a second grade system." Quine, *Ontological Relativity and Other Essays* (New York: Columbia University Press, 1969), p. 24.

17. See Bernard Williams, *Descartes: The Project of Pure Enquiry* (Harmondsworth: Penguin, 1978) and *Ethics and the Limits of Philosophy* (Cambridge, Mass.: Harvard University Press, 1985).

18. Simon Blackburn, *Spreading the Word: Groundings in the Philosophy of Language* (Oxford: Clarendon Press, 1984) and *Essays in Quasi-Realism* (Oxford: Oxford University Press, 1993).

19. "The worry about propositional attitudes is that they are too much like (the avowedly nonexistent) phlogiston, caloric, and the four principles of medieval alchemy." From p. 2 in Paul Churchland's "Activation Vectors versus Propositional Attitudes: How the Brain Represents Reality," *Philosophy and Phenomenological Research*, 52, no. 2 (June 1992), pp. 1–6. I reply to Churchland in "Truth, Activation Vectors, and Possession Conditions for Concepts," ibid., pp. 431–447.

NOTES TO PART II

1. The Three Enlightenments

1. Plato, *Euthyphro*. The translation I quote from is that of Lane Cooper, in Edith Hamilton and Huntington Cairns, eds., *Plato:*

The Collected Dialogues (Princeton: Princeton University Press, 1961), pp. 169–185. I have rectified the translation by using "pious" and "impious" (in agreement with the majority of translations) where Lane Cooper has "holy" and "unholy."

2. The seminal work of John Rawls, in particular his celebrated *A Theory of Justice* (Cambridge, Mass.: Harvard University Press, 1971), is largely responsible for this.

3. I take the notion of "capabilities" from Amartya Sen. Sen has developed the "capabilities approach" in a series of publications, stretching as far back as his *Commodities and Capabilities* (Amsterdam: North-Holland, 1985) and *Ethics and Economics* (Oxford: Blackwell, 1987). A recent major statement is his *Development as Freedom* (New York: Random House, 1999).

4. See Brinton's article "Enlightenment" in *The Encyclopedia of Philosophy* (New York: Crowell, Collier and Macmillan, 1967), vol. 2. I quote from p. 519.

5. Ibid., p. 519.

6. *Republic,* V. 454–455. I am using F. M. Cornford's translation, *The Republic of Plato* (Oxford: Oxford University Press, 1945).

7. Ibid.

8. Plato does say, in agreement with common (male) Greek opinion, that "as a whole" the men are more gifted than the women (V. 455), but immediately after making *this* concession, he insists that "there is no occupation concerned with the management of social affairs which belongs either to woman or to man as such. Natural gifts are to be found here and there in both creatures alike; and every occupation is open to both, so far as their natures are concerned, although woman is for all purposes the weaker."

9. Contrary to Marxist critics, however, this is not an exploitative society in Marx's sense, because there is supposed to be little or no social surplus. In fact, Plato's ideal republic is in many ways like a Gandhian *ashram.*

10. *Experience and Nature,* volume 1 (1925) of Jo Ann Boydston, ed., *The Later Works of John Dewey* (Carbondale: Southern Illinois University Press, 1981–1990), p. 298.

11. Dewey and Tufts, *Ethics,* volume 7 (1932) of Jo Ann Boydston, ed., *The Later Works of John Dewey* (Carbondale: Southern Illinois University Press, 1981–1990), p. 347.

12. Robert B. Westbrook, *John Dewey and American Democracy* (Ithaca, N.Y.: Cornell University Press, 1991).

13. William James, *Essays in Radical Empiricism,* ed. F. Bowers and I. J. Skrupskelis (Cambridge, Mass.: Harvard University Press, 1994), p. 16.

14. Ruth Anna Putnam and I have argued that Dewey's *Logic, the Theory of Inquiry,* which as its subtitle indicates is a general theory of *inquiry,* and not what philosophers today call "logic," is to be read as a reply to and rebuttal of Mill's *System of Logic;* and that both books are concerned with the question "What is the right method of inquiry into social problems?" See our "Epistemology as Hypothesis," *Transactions of the Charles S. Peirce Society,* 26, no. 4 (Fall 1990), pp. 407–434; collected in my *Words and Life* (Cambridge, Mass.: Harvard University Press, 1994), under the title "Dewey's *Logic:* Epistemology as Hypothesis." *Logic* is volume 12 (1938) in Jo Ann Boydston, ed., *The Later Works of John Dewey* (Carbondale: Southern Illinois University Press, 1981–1990).

15. I refer, of course, to the notorious proof of "The Falling Rate of Profit." It may be objected that the proof is not *wholly* a priori; Marx does need the empirical assumption of "the increasing organic composition of capital." But he offers not one shred of *evidence* for this assumption!

16. Brinton, "Enlightenment," p. 519.

17. This quotation is from the 1908 edition of Dewey and Tufts, *Ethics,* volume 5 in Jo Ann Boydston, ed., *The Middle Works of John Dewey* (Carbondale: Southern Illinois University Press, 1976–1983), pp. 271–272 (a section written by Dewey).

18. Rawls's defense of a social contract model in *A Theory of Justice* is meant to avoid this objection by deriving the model from our idea of "Fairness." Such a purely conceptual defense seems to me to be inconsistent with Rawls's repudiation of the "conceptual analysis" conception of moral philosophy, however. Talk of "reflective equilibrium" looks suspiciously like a way of trying to have your cake and eat it too!

19. See Dewey's *The Public and Its Problems,* included in volume 2 (1925–1927) of Jo Ann Boydston, ed., *The Later Works of John Dewey* (Carbondale: Southern Illinois University Press, 1981–1990).

20. See H. Putnam and R. A. Putnam, "Epistemology as Hypothesis."

21. John Rawls, *Lectures on the History of Moral Philosophy* (Cambridge, Mass.: Harvard University Press, 2000), pp. 8–11.

2. Skepticism about Enlightenment

1. The impulse to reflective transcendence is closely related to what Habermas calls "the emancipatory interest" in *Erkenntnis und Interesse* (translated into English as *Knowledge and Human Interests* [Boston: Beacon Press, 1971]).

2. This is a view that was popularized by A. J. Ayer (*Philosophical Essays* [London, 1959], p. 237) when he wrote that "what are accounted reasons for our moral judgments are reasons only in the sense that they determine attitudes." Ayer was following Rudolf Carnap, who was willing to allow ethical judgments to have meaning only in the sense that "conceptions and images" can be associated with them—something which, Carnap said, is true of "any arbitrarily compounded series of words" (*The Unity of Science* [London: Kegan Paul, Trench, Hubner, 1934], pp. 26–27). The logical positivists indeed believed that they had given a logical analysis of *all* possible kinds of cognitively meaningful judgments, and that analysis showed that value judgments could not have "cognitive meaning." Today the positivist theory of cognitive meaning is generally recognized to have been a failure. (See my book cited in note 3 below for details.)

3. Hilary Putnam, *The Collapse of the Fact/Value Dichotomy* (Cambridge, Mass.: Harvard University Press, 2002).

4. I do not find this second form (described below as the idea of a bottomless regress of interpretations) in Foucault.

5. An example is Ian Hacking's beautiful study, *The Emergence of Probability* (Cambridge: Cambridge University Press, 1975). Another is Arnold I. Davidson, "Structures and Strategies of Discourse: Remarks Toward a History of Foucault's Philosophy of Language," in A. I. Davidson, ed., *Foucault and His Interlocutors* (Chicago: University of Chicago Press, 1996).

6. *Reason, Truth, and History* (Cambridge: Cambridge University Press, 1981), pp. 156–158.

7. Ibid., pp. 157–158.

8. Rorty, "Putnam and the Relativist Menace," *The Journal of Philosophy,* 90, no. 9 (September 1993), p. 450.

9. For references see my *Renewing Philosophy* (Cambridge, Mass.: Harvard University Press, 1992), p. 218, n. 22.

10. Charles Travis, *Unshadowed Thought* (Cambridge, Mass.: Harvard University Press, 2000), p. 129.

11. See Travis, *Unshadowed Thought,* and Martin Stone, "Focusing the Law: What Legal Interpretation Is Not," in Andrei Marmor, ed., *Law and Interpretation: Essays in Legal Philosophy* (Oxford: Oxford University Press, 1995), pp. 31–95.

12. Christopher Mortensen, "Plato's Pharmacy and Derrida's Drugstore," *Language and Communication,* 20 (2000), pp. 329–346.

13. See "Deconstruction and Circumvention," in Rorty's *Essays on Heidegger and Others,* vol. 2 of *Philosophical Papers* (Cambridge: Cambridge University Press, 1991), pp. 93–94, n. 12.

14. Stone, "Focusing the Law," p. 55. For a more detailed analysis of "deconstructionist" readings of Wittgenstein and a comparison/contrast of Wittgenstein and Derrida, see also Stone's "Wittgenstein and Deconstruction" in Alice Crary and Rupert Read, eds., *The New Wittgenstein* (London: Routledge, 2000).

15. For instance, the term "Postmodernism" itself, as if this were an epoch on a par with Modernism or Romanticism or Enlightenment.

16. However, I mistakenly classified it as "cultural relativism" in that essay: "Why Realism Can't Be Naturalized," in my *Realism and Reason,* vol. 3 of *Philosophical Papers* (Cambridge: Cambridge University Press, 1983), pp. 230–240.

17. *Rorty and His Critics,* ed. Robert Brandom (Oxford: Blackwell, 2000).

18. Bernard Williams, "Philosophy as a Humanistic Discipline," *Philosophy,* 75 (2000), pp. 477–495.

19. Ibid., p. 487.

20. Ibid., pp. 487–488.

21. Ibid., p. 486.

22. By the way, the philosophy of science in this passage is naïve: if quantum mechanics "explains" phenomena, it does so in a sense of "explain" that would have been as alien to the ways of thinking of a classical physicist as talk of "the rights of man" would have been to someone living in the *ancien régime.* Quantum mechanics has no single accepted interpretation to the present day. Thus it does not (at present) "explain" a single phenomenon in the classic sense of providing a dynamical picture which accounts for it. What it does instead is *redescribe phenomena in terms of structures which are utterly abstract*—not structures in space-time, but such set-theoretic objects as projection operators on Hilbert spaces. And the sense in which the classical theories it replaces are "limiting cases" of quantum mechanics is likewise novel (treating Poisson brackets as limiting cases of entirely different mathematical expressions which have formal similarities to them). In fact, we could write, mimicking Williams, "For quantum-mechanical ideas to have won an argument, classical physicists would have had to have shared with the nascent quantum physicists a conception of something that the argument was about, and not just in the obvious sense that it was about physical phenomena. They would have had to agree that there was some aim, of explanation or correct description or whatever, which quantum mechanical ideas served better or of which they were a better expression, and there is not much reason, with a change as radical as this, to think that they did agree about this, at least until late in the process. The relevant ideas of explanation, description, and so on were themselves involved in the change."

23. Williams, "Philosophy as a Humanistic Discipline," p. 488.

24. Ibid., p. 490.

25. See Menachem Fisch, *Rational Rabbis* (Bloomington: Indiana University Press, 1997).

26. In "The Fixation of Belief," collected in *The Collected Papers of Charles Sanders Peirce,* vol. 5, ed. Charles Hartshorne and Paul Weiss (Cambridge, Mass.: Harvard University Press, 1960), pp. 223–247. The quotation is from p. 242 (§383).

27. E.g., in Rorty, *Contingency, Irony, and Solidarity* (Cambridge: Cambridge University Press, 1989).

28. Williams, "Philosophy as a Humanistic Discipline," pp. 490–491.

29. Notably in "Solidarity or Objectivity?", in *Post-Analytic Philosophy*, ed. John Rajchman and Cornel West (New York: Columbia University Press, 1985).

Index